編者的話

　　由於學習環境的限制，使得國人在英文寫作方面的訓練，稍嫌不足。如社交、求職、留學信函之類的日常應用文體，普遍令大眾不知所措。有鑑於此，本公司特編成「**新應用英文範例**」(*Practical English Writing*)一書，作為讀者書寫時的指南。其特色有：

♥ **包羅廣泛・分類清楚** —— 除傳統書信之外，亦收錄了履歷表 (Resume)、傳真(Fax)、卡片(Card)、通知(Announcement)、啓事(Notice) ……多種應用文體。全書採系統的分類方法，將日常的英語應用文體歸為八大類，一目了然，方便查詢。

◆ **範文齊全・內容實用** —— 針對日常生活可能發生的情況，設計各類範文，每一篇都能切合讀者的需求。本書英文內容，悉由外籍人士撰寫，無論在風格或語法上，都是 100 % 的英文。

♠ **註解詳盡・語句活用** —— 於範文後詳註生字、詞彙，並附中譯，減少閱讀障礙。**Useful Expressions** 提供多樣句型，讓您靈活運用，增添文章色彩，賦予文章新生命。

♣ **精彩附錄・方便查詢** —— 本書內含許多實用附錄，如在情書部份，有大文豪的不朽情話；留學信函中，有留學小情報；貿易書信內，有商用專有名詞……節省讀者查詢資料的時間。

　　本書秉承學習的一貫傳統，從策畫、撰寫、校訂，乃至版面的設計，莫不力求盡善盡美。然疏漏之處恐在所難免，尚祈各界先進不吝賜教與斧正。

Editorial Staff

- 編著 / 吳濱伶

- 校訂 / 劉　毅・陳瑠琍・謝靜芳
　　　　蔡琇瑩・劉復苓

- 校閱 / Barbara Gilbert・Thomas Deneau

- 封面設計 / 高文志・張鳳儀

- 版面設計 / 張鳳儀・高文志

- 版面構成 / 高文志・張瓊惠

- 完稿 / 張鳳儀・吳正順

- 打字 / 黃淑貞・倪秀梅・吳秋香

CONTENTS

Chapter 3
工作類信函

Chapter 4
學校類信函

Chapter 5
貿易書信

英文書信概論

　　應用文涵蓋的範圍相當廣泛，從私人信件、公函、請柬，到電報、傳真等，都囊括在內。舉凡人與人之間往來時，所使用特定形式的文字，經社會約定俗成共通使用，都稱為應用文。由於國情迥異，英語應用文的格式與禮節，和中文都不盡相同。在本書的第一章，我們將就最普及的應用文類——書信，作深入淺出的介紹。首先，我們來談談書信的常識，接著再從書信的七大結構作焦點式的介紹，最末一單元，我們會說明信封的格式。相信您在讀完本章後，應當能對英文書信有更深入的認識。

Unit 1 ▶ 英文書信常識

　　有人覺得提筆寫信頗難，畢竟文字不夠真實，用來表情達意，常有落差出現。儘管如此，書信的價值仍不可小覷。對口才拙劣的人而言，透過文字來溝通，也許能更清楚的傳達思想；不少人因為害羞，愛你在心「口」難開，往往也需藉書信來吐露愛意。

　　中國人特重禮節，在稱謂、提稱語……等書信結構方面，分類細密，讓人不易掌握。相較之下，英文書信的格式就顯得容易。倘若能熟悉格式的重點，再運用巧思，配上充實、達意的內容，一封文情並茂的英文書信便可產生。在此一單元，我們先為讀者概略地介紹英文書信的常識，引領您進入書信的繽紛世界。

書寫工具

　　隨著打字機與電腦的普及，愈來愈多的書信以打字代替手寫。打字可免去字跡潦草、看不清的困擾，又能使書信看起來整齊美觀。大致來說，業務信件常用打字，而私人信件仍多用手寫，以示親切。

　　書寫用的墨水以**黑色**或**藍黑色**為宜，避免使用鮮豔的墨色。綠墨水是熱戀中的情侶所用，而紅墨水有輕蔑之意，多用在絕交信。以鉛筆來書寫極不禮貌，若沒有合適的工具替代，也應該在後面加上 *Please excuse my writing with a pencil.* 表示歉意。

信紙

　　業務信件多用打字，因此有特定用紙，一般的規格是 $8\frac{1}{2} \times 11$ 吋，或 8×10 吋，至於手寫用的信紙則形形色色。原則上，無論何種信件，

都宜選用**無線條**、**白色或素色**、**品質良好**的信紙來書寫。紙的磅數愈高，品質愈佳，但航空信紙例外。由於航空郵資不便宜，使用輕薄的航空信紙，將可減少花費。

　　信件內容若超過一張，應另起新頁，不可在背後繼續書寫，同時也必須標明頁數，方便他人閱讀。若採用折疊信紙（Double Letter），須注意書寫順序。請參考下圖：

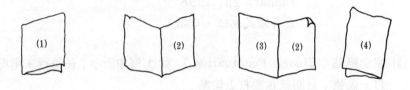

書信格式

　　信文與信封的寫法可略分為鋸齒式、齊頭式、折衷式、完全標點與簡略標點。鋸齒式與完全標點為傳統的書信模式，也稱作英國式，而齊頭式與簡略標點是因應打字機而產生，又稱美國式。兩者的不同，只是外形上的差異而已。也有將這兩種方法合併的折衷式，在使用上相當受到歡迎。

1. 鋸齒式（Indented Style）：信封或信文內的姓名、地址、日期等項目，每一行逐列斜向縮排一、二個字母。正文部份每段的首行從左側向右縮進三～五個字母。結尾謙辭、署名寫在信紙右下方。

> 8, Lane 505,
> 　Chung Shan N. Rd., Sec. 5,
> 　　Taipei, Taiwan,
> 　　　R.O.C.,
> 　　　　October 26, 1994.
> （鋸齒式地址、日期）

2 **齊頭式**（ Block Style ）：不論是地址、正文……結尾謙辭、署名，每行均齊頭排列。這種樣式不易分出區段，所以必須在各段之間留些空白。

> 3F-1, 65, Lane 63
> Tunhua S. Rd., Sec.2
> Taipei, Taiwan
> R.O.C.
> January 25, 1998
> （ 齊頭式地址、日期 ）

3 **完全標點**（ Closed Punctuation ）：如1例中所示，在每行末尾均打上逗號，日期後也要打上句點。

4 **簡略標點**（ Open Punctuation ）：如2例中所示，每行末均省略標點符號，日期後的句點也不寫，但是各行中的逗號與縮寫標點仍需保留。

5 **折衷式**（ Semi-block ）：信文中的寄信人地址、日期，收信人姓名、地址兩欄用齊頭式，而正文、結尾謙辭、署名用鋸齒式。信封上的寄信人地址用齊頭式，收信人地址用鋸齒式。

Unit 2 ▸ 英文書信結構

　　書信的結構主要分爲七部份：(1) 寄信人地址、日期，(2) 收信人姓名、地址，(3) 稱謂，(4) 正文，(5) 結尾謙辭，(6) 署名，(7) 再啓，其在信紙上的相關位置如下圖所示：

(1) 寄信人地址、日期
(Heading)

(2) 收信人姓名、地址
(Inside Address)

(3) 稱謂(Salutation)

(4) 正文
(Body of the Letter)

(5) 結尾謙辭
(Complimentary Close)

(6) 署名(Signature)

(7) 再啓(P.S. , Postscript)

寄信人地址、日期 (*Heading*)

　　寄信人地址、日期一欄，位於信紙的**右上角**。書寫地址的目的，是讓收信人知道信的來源，而日期則是表明發信的時間。寄給親密好友的信件，簡略寫個地名即可；而機關行號多有自用信箋，上頭印有 Letterhead（含名稱、地址、電話等），使用時，只需在 Letterhead 下方、靠信紙中央或右半部的位置，填上日期。

Learning Publishing Co., Ltd.
4F, 11, Lane 200, Tunghwa St., Taipei, Taiwan
Tel: (02) 704-5525　　Fax: (02) 707-9095

May 5, 1998

　　地址的寫法是由小地方到大地方，可採用美國式或英國式（請參考前一單元）。日期的寫法也分英式與美式兩種，英國式是按照日（多用序數）、月、年的順序，而美式寫法則先寫月份、次寫日期、然後是年份。由於兩者的差異易產生混淆，**應避免簡寫**。再者，月份也宜完整拼出，不要使用縮寫。

英式日期：1st April, 1995（簡寫爲 1/4/95）
美式日期：April 1, 1995　（簡寫爲 4/1/95）

門牌號碼──────→	4F, 11, Lane 200
街道名稱──────→	Tunghwa St.
城　　市──────→	Taipei, Taiwan
國　　名──────→	R.O.C.
日　　期──────→	October 10, 1995

（美式地址寫法）

收信人姓名、地址 (*Inside Address*)

收信人姓名與地址寫於信紙的**左上方**，比日期約低一、二行。第一行先寫姓名，若有單位名稱，寫在第二行，再下才接地址，寫法和前述相同。業務書信中，此欄宜詳細書寫，若寫給親朋好友，則可省略。

英語姓名的寫法是先寫名字 (first name)，再寫姓氏 (surname)。姓名的開頭字母均要大寫，前面需加上稱號。以下是各類稱號的用法：

1. **男性單數**：可用 Mr. (Mister 簡寫) 或 Esq. (Esquire 簡寫)。Mr. 需放在姓名之前，如 Mr. Jeff Hoffman，而 Esq. 放在姓氏後，前面得加逗號，如 Jeff Hoffman, Esq.。

2. **男性複數**：對男性複數稱 Messrs. (法文 Messieurs 的略語)，男女混合團體也可用 Messrs.。

3. **女性單數**：稱未婚女子用 Miss，已婚婦女是 Mrs.，若不清楚其婚姻狀況，可折衷使用 Ms.。

4. **女性複數**：對婦女團體使用 Mesdames，或簡寫的 Mmes.。

5. **特殊頭銜**：若已知收信人的頭銜，宜稱呼其頭銜，而不用一般稱號，如 Dr. John King。以下是常用的職銜簡寫：

> Dr. = Doctor （博士、醫生）　　Prof. = Professor （教授）
> Gen. = General （將軍）　　　　Capt. = Captain （船長）
> Gov. = Governor （省長、州長）　Amb. = Ambassador （大使）

稱謂 (*Salutation*)

稱謂自成一行，寫在 Inside Address 下方約二行處，並與之齊頭。稱謂的用法因人數、性別、與親疏關係而不同，請參照下表：

對象	英　　式	美　　式	註
團體	Dear Sirs, Dear Mesdames,	Gentlemen： Ladies：	一般公司團體 女性團體
男性	Sir, Dear Sir, Dear Mr. S, My Dear F,	Sir： Dear Sir： Dear Mr. S： Dear F：	正　式 一　般 熟　識 親　密
女性	Madam, Dear Madam, Dear Mrs.或 Miss S, My Dear F,	Madam： Dear Madam： Dear Mrs.或 Miss S： Dear F：	正　式 一　般 熟　識 親　密

➡ F 表名字（First name），S 表姓（Surname）。

正文 (Body)

　　上述的結構，以及結尾謙辭等，都屬於格式的範疇，只需依情況作適當的選擇，正文才是真正需要心思與技巧的部份。日常書信往來，公、私函的比例各半，雖然私人信件可不必太拘謹，但內容也不能雜蕪無章，流於隨便。正文的書寫有幾項原則：

1. **準確**（Correctness）：準確是最重要的一環。收信人可能不認識你，更不清楚來信的用意，因此有必要將相關事宜，據實寫出，讓對方了解。

2. **簡潔**（Conciseness）：現代人生活分秒必爭，無暇細讀長篇大論。因此，寄信人必須開門見山，將事情簡潔、清楚地交代，首先說明來信的用意，接著陳述重要事實，最後交代收信人應有的回應。

3 **禮貌**（Courtesy）：所謂禮貌是站在對方的立場，將其心理、處境、與習慣列入考量，而非用華麗的辭藻來裝飾。寄到國外的信件，尤其得注意禮節的差異，以免貽笑大方。

4 **清楚**（Clarity）：寫信的目的不在賣弄學問，所以應避免使用艱澀的辭彙，以及冗長的語句。適度的分段，可讓僵硬的紙面看來活潑，也方便收信人閱讀。

結尾謙辭 *(Complimentary Close)*

結尾謙辭相當於中文的「敬上」，是寫信人對收信人的謙稱。使用鋸齒式與折衷式的格式，結尾謙辭、署名需寫在正文的右下方，在齊頭式中，則與信文齊頭。結尾謙辭**開頭的字母須大寫**，末尾要加逗號。依寄信人與收信人的關係，結尾謙辭的用法可分以下幾種：

✦ 一般用法
　Yours truly, Truly yours,
　Yours sincerely, Sincerely yours,

✦ 給機關行號或陌生人
　Yours truly, Truly yours,
　Yours sincerely, Sincerely yours,

✦ 給在上位者或長輩
　Yours respectfully, Respectfully yours,
　Yours obediently, Obediently yours,

✦ 親人摯友、情侶夫妻
　Love, With love,
　Lovingly, Lovingly yours,
　Yours affectionately, Affectionately yours,
　Your loving *son*（child, daughter, sister, grandmother…）

署名 (*Signature*)

　　傳統署名的位置緊接在結尾謙辭之下。署名須**親筆書寫**，即使用打字，仍需加上親筆簽名，且不可附帶稱號。但若是名字不易讓人分辨出性別，或是女性為表明身份，可利用**括號**附記上**Mr.、Mrs.** 或 **Miss**，如：

(Miss) Sidney Schmidt

再啓 (*P.S., Postscript*)

　　信件寫完，發現有事忘了交代，可在署名下一行，靠左端部份寫上 P.S.，補述遺漏的事。P.S. 之後毋須再簽名，但若是重大事情，則在其後簽上姓名的字首（ Initials ）。再啓的方式不甚禮貌，應避免濫用。

1050 Benton St.
Apt. #1208
Santa Clara, CA 95050
U.S.A.
February 14, 1998

Mr. Stevie Wu
8, Lane 505
Chung Shan N. Road Sec. 5
Taipei, Taiwan
R.O.C.

Dear Stevie,

I have such good news that I could hardly wait to tell you. Jane finally agreed to marry me. We are getting married on June 7 in the Methodist Church down the road from our old school. For our honeymoon we are thinking of spending a week in Taiwan. If you have time, could you show us around Taipei and suggest some scenic spots for us to visit in Taiwan? We would both be very grateful. I am awaiting your reply.

Yours sincerely,

Jimmy

P.S. Please give my regards to your parents and Grandmother.

(折衷式書信)

Unit 3 ▶ 信封格式

　　信封上需填寫的部份有(1)收信人姓名、地址,(2)寄信人姓名、地址,(3)郵遞指示,(4)收信指示,(5)郵票等項目,相關位置請見下圖:

Stevie Wu
8, Lane 505　(2)
Chung Shan N. Rd., Sec. 5
Taipei, Taiwan

(5)

　　　　　　　　　　　　Mr. Sam Korsmoe
　　　　　　　　　　　　110 Collis Ave.　(1)
AIRMAIL (3)　　　　Los Angeles CA 90259
　　　　　　　　　　　　U.S.A.

Private (4)

　　收信人姓名、地址寫在信封的**中央**或是**右下**四分之一處。郵票貼在右上角,超過一張時,由右往左貼,然後再往下。寄信人的姓名、地址寫於**左上方**,或是信封的背面,但一般認爲前者較適宜。

　　郵遞指示可註明在信封**顯眼處**,常見的有 By Air Mail 或 Par Avion（航空信）, Express（快遞）, Prompt Delivery（限時專送）, Registered（掛號）, Printed Matter（印刷品）等。收信指示可標於信封左下方,如 Private , Personal , Confidential 等均表「親啓」; Rush , Immediate , 或 Urgent 表示「急件」。

地址的寫法

　　地址的寫法如第一單元所示，可採鋸齒式或齊頭式，完全標點或簡略標點。收信人的地址只需依照來信者的寫法，門牌街名宜完整拼出，而州、省的名稱也一定要寫，因為在不同的州（省），常有同名的街道。至於寄信人地址，則可參考台灣的英文地址的寫法。

Rm. = Room （室）	F = Floor （樓）	Aly. = Alley （弄）
Ln. = Lane （巷）	Sec. = Section （段）	N. = North （北）
S. = South （南）	W. = West （西）	E. = East （東）
St. = Street （街）	Rd. = Road （路）	Township （鎮）
Town （鄉）	Village （村）	County （縣）

信紙的摺法

　　信紙不宜摺疊多次，以免損壞外形。使用小信封時，將信文朝內對摺，再分三等分摺疊二次（如圖一示）。若是大信封，則分三等分來摺（如圖二示）。

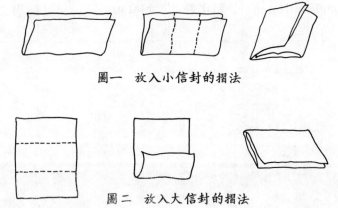

圖一　放入小信封的摺法

圖二　放入大信封的摺法

台灣縣市名稱英譯

Taipei City	台北市	Yunlin Hsien	雲林縣
Kaohsiung City	高雄市	Chiayi Hsien	嘉義縣
Taichung City	台中市	Tainan Hsien	台南縣
Tainan City	台南市	Kaohsiung Hsien	高雄縣
Keelung City	基隆市	Pingtung Hsien	屏東縣
Hsinchu City	新竹市	Yilan Hsien	宜蘭縣
Chiayi City	嘉義市	Hualian Hsien	花蓮縣
Taipei Hsien	台北縣	Taitung Hsien	台東縣
Taoyuan Hsien	桃園縣	Nantou Hsien	南投縣
Hsinchu Hsien	新竹縣	Penghu Hsien	澎湖縣
Miaoli Hsien	苗栗縣	Makung	馬　公
Taichung Hsien	台中縣	Kinmen（Quemoy）	金　門
Changhwa Hsien	彰化縣	Matsu	馬　祖

＊縣可使用 County 或音譯的 Hsien 。

社交類信函

　　日常書信往來中，以社交信函最爲常見。不論是婚喪喜慶時的交際應酬，抑或親朋好友間的情感聯絡，書信都不失爲一個好工具。然而各民族間有其獨特的表達方式，若以中國人的觀點來概括其他民族的想法，則不免有疏失。因此，在提筆寫信給外國友人時，除了體例要恰當，內容也宜符合西方的禮儀。本章將社交信函分爲祝賀、邀請、問候、通知、慰問、弔唁、道歉、致謝、情書等九大類，除提供實用的書信範例外，並概略地介紹各類社交信函的禮儀，以作爲讀者書寫時的參考。

社交信函禮儀

祝賀（*Congratulations*）

　　當友人欣逢喜事，寄上我們的祝福，不但是種禮貌，更可顯出我們的誠意。祝賀信不必冗長，只要是發自內心的祝福，簡短數句即可。市面上雖有各類賀卡，但是親筆致賀，會令收信者倍感溫馨。況且卡片中的賀詞良莠不齊，挑選時得格外謹慎。祝賀信函注重時效，在獲悉消息後，即應儘快寄出。

邀請（*Invitations*）

　　邀請函可分正式與非正式兩種。非正式的邀請函常用於小型聚會、私人飯局，和一般信件相同，皆以第一人稱書寫。語氣上要誠懇、客氣，時間與地點亦需說明清楚，以方便受邀者回覆。回函應及早寄出，讓主人有充裕的時間作處理。答覆要明確，千萬不可用「如果有空，我一定會到」等模稜兩可的話。接受邀請應感謝主人的盛情邀約，若因故無法參加，也要委婉的解釋理由，並致上歉意。

　　正式的邀請函常使用精美的雕刻印刷，以第三人稱書寫。第一行寫主人的名字，第二行可用 request the pleasure of *one's* company 之類的邀請語，接下才寫事由。正式的回函也須採用相同格式，接受邀請可用「受邀者＋accept with pleasure ～」的句型。若婉辭邀請則用「受邀者＋regret that〔they are〕unable to accept ～」（括號中的部份視情況作變化）。

問候（*Tidings*）

　　問候信是親朋好友、筆友間往來的書信。由於彼此認識，書寫時不必過於嚴肅與拘謹，只需以平時說話的口吻，向對方描述生活的點滴，以及周遭人們的消息。問候信可增進情誼，應該常常書寫，與外國筆友通信，不但能增進英文能力，也能認識更多的異國文化。

慰問（*Sympathy*）

　　人在失意或病痛中，格外需要安慰與鼓勵。適時的寄上慰問信函，除表達溫馨的情誼，也讓病人或失意者為之振奮。慰問信應多提及人生的光明面，讓收信者覺得世界充滿希望。此外，也需盡己力伸出援手，幫他們渡過難關。

弔唁（*Condolences*）

　　弔唁信難度最高，但也是最需要寫的信函。信中除了安慰遺屬，也可表達對死者的感懷，頌揚逝者的勳業。內容宜**簡短、真誠**，切忌引起悲傷的字眼。至於該寫信給誰，視情況而定。若認識的是死者，應寫給死者最親的人，也可在收信人後面加上 and the family。若只認識死者的親屬，則直接寄給所認識的人。

道歉（*Apologies*）

　　人都不免為了疏失，必須向人道歉，然而因為面子問題，常難以啟齒，這時就可利用信函來道歉。道歉信需**立刻寫**，否則即失去作用。若是無心之過，不妨稍作解釋，但不宜將責任推得一乾二淨，以免引起反感。如果過錯在己，應坦誠無諱，並表示不再犯。若有必要，應該設法補救，賠償損失。

致謝（*Gratitude*）

許多場合需要謝函，為示誠意，宜親筆書寫，語氣也應誠懇，寫完盡早寄出。

謝弔唁：弔唁謝函由收信人回覆，但若遺屬過於悲慟，由其他親屬或朋友代筆也無妨。回函不必急著寄出，但也不宜超過六個星期，內容宜簡短。假使收到的慰問信太多，無暇一一答謝，可使用卡片代替。

謝賀禮：收到賀函或賀禮，得盡快寄出謝函，內容不必冗言，可提及生活近況或禮物用途。結婚賀禮由新娘負責回謝，每收到禮物就該立刻寄出謝函，不宜等禮物堆積如山，才以卡片代替。

謝款待：接受晚宴招待後，應寫信向**女主人**致謝，若能點出最喜歡的菜餚或節目，可使謝函看起來更具說服力。

情書（*Love Letter*）

情書是傳達愛意的最佳工具，利用英文寫情書，可使人一改平日的保守，流露熱情。情書著重**真情**，而非辭藻的堆砌，只要發自內心，都能寫出雋永感人的情書。情書必須**親筆書寫**，字跡醜陋不打緊，重要的是讓對方明瞭你的用心與誠意。對新交往的朋友，不宜表現得太露骨，即使雙方關係親密，語氣也不能輕浮。在稱謂上，可選用My Darling，My dearest～，My Sweetheart（通常指女性）等親暱的稱呼。

祝賀生日

October 26, 1998

Dear Mark,

    Congratulations on your birthday and I wish you many happy returns. I hope you enjoy all your presents and make full use of this opportunity to be with your family and friends. It is said that to grow older is to grow wiser, in this case I hope you will have many more such birthdays.

Affectionately yours,

1998年10月26日

親愛的馬克：

    生日快樂！祝你福如東海，壽比南山。希望你喜歡所有的禮物，並能充分藉此機會，與家人及朋友相聚。有人說，智慧是年齡的累積，所以，我祝你能度過更多這般的生日。

敬上

＊＊ 祝賀他人常用「congratulations on＋事由」的句型。
    congratulation 用複數形。

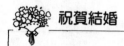 **祝賀結婚**

May 5, 1998

Dear Michael,

It is with great pleasure that I congratulate you on your marriage. While some of your friends doubted this day would ever arrive, I always knew you and Anna made the perfect pair.

On this happiest of days I would like to wish you both a long and happy life together as well as a prosperous future.

Your friend,

** prosperous〔'prɑspərəs〕 *adj.* 興隆的

Marriage

1998 年 5 月 5 日

親愛的麥克：

　　滿心歡喜地恭喜你結婚了。雖然有些朋友懷疑這天會不會到來，然而我一直清楚，你和安娜是天造地設的一對。

　　在這最快樂的日子裡，我祝福你倆白頭偕老，幸福美滿。

友

♥ 結婚紀念日名稱①

the paper wedding anniversary	紙　婚	（ 1 年）
the straw wedding anniversary	蒭　婚	（ 2 年）
the candy wedding anniversary	糖　婚	（ 3 年）
the leather wedding anniversary	革　婚	（ 4 年）
the wooden wedding anniversary	木　婚	（ 5 年）
the floral wedding anniversary	花　婚	（ 7 年）
the tin wedding anniversary	錫　婚	（10 年）
the linen wedding anniversary	亞麻婚	（12 年）

 祝賀結婚周年紀念

June 22, 1998

Dear Sophia and Joseph,

On your silver wedding anniversary, I would like to extend my warmest congratulations. While a quarter of a century may have passed, I still remember the two of you as the perfect couple at your wedding.

At this important moment I wish you both another twenty-five years of blissful harmony together.

Love,

** anniversary〔͵ænə′vɝsərɪ〕 *n.* 周年紀念
　blissful〔′blɪsfəl〕 *adj.* 幸福的
　harmony〔′hɑrmənɪ〕 *n.* 融洽

Wedding Anniversary

1998年6月22日

親愛的蘇菲亞及約瑟夫：

　　欣逢你們銀婚紀念日，我想要致上最誠摯的祝賀之意。縱然四分之一個世紀已經過去了，我仍記得在婚禮上，你們這對天造地設的佳偶。

　　在這重要的時刻，我祝福你倆，共度另一個琴瑟和鳴的二十五年。

敬上

● 結婚紀念日名稱②

the crystal wedding anniversary	水晶婚（15 年）
the china wedding anniversary	陶　婚（20 年）
the silver wedding anniversary	銀　婚（25 年）
the pearl wedding anniversary	珍珠婚（30 年）
the coral wedding anniversary	珊瑚婚（35 年）
the emerald wedding anniversary	翡翠婚（40 年）
the ruby wedding anniversary	紅玉婚（45 年）
the gold(en) wedding anniversary	金　婚（50 年）
the diamond wedding anniversary	鑽石婚（60 年）

 祝賀生產

January 1，1998

Dear Mrs. Connor,

I am sending you this note to congratulate you on the birth of your son. I hope that you and your son are fine and that you will recover quickly. Because of this happy event, you and your husband must be very proud indeed.

Cordially yours,

1998年1月1日

親愛的康諾太太：

寄上這封短箋，恭喜你喜獲麟兒。希望你們母子均安好，你也能快速復原。因為這樁喜事，你和你先生一定感到驕傲萬分。

敬上

祝賀喬遷

September 23, 1998

Dear Jonathan,

    I was happy to hear that you had found a new house, as the old one wasn't really suitable for you. I hope the new house is more convenient to your lifestyle and that you will be very happy there.

    Do write to me and tell me all about the new house. If you are having a house warming party, do tell me as soon as possible.

Your friend,

1998年9月23日

親愛的強納生：

    眞高興你找到了新房子，原來的房子實在不適合你。但願這新居對你的生活方式更便利，也希望你住得愉快。

    記得寫信告訴我新房子的一切，如果你要辦喬遷宴會，及早通知我。

友

祝賀金榜題名

August 25, 1998

Dear Sean,

　　I was most pleased to hear that you passed your examination and that you did so well. I, and all of your friends, always knew you had it in you. After so much effort and hard work my advice to you is to relax for a while and enjoy the fruit of your labor. I hope we can get together some time; please drop me a line soon.

　　　　　　　　　　　　　　　　Your friend,

Passing an Examination

1998 年 8 月 25 日

親愛的席恩：

聽到你金榜題名且表現優異，我真是欣喜萬分。我、以及你所有的朋友，一直都知道你深藏不露。經過這麼多的奮鬥與努力，我給你的建議是好好休息一下，並且享受努力的成果。希望我們能找時間聚聚，也請你儘快回信。

友

NOTES

1 *have it in one* 指具有某方面才能，但卻不為人知。

2 *drop sb. a line*〔*note*〕 寄短信

USEFUL EXPRESSIONS

* Congratulations on your success in the entrance exam.
  恭喜你入學考金榜題名。

* When I saw your name on the pass-list, I wanted to be the first to congratulate you.
  看到你的名字上榜，我想第一個恭喜你。

祝賀畢業暨就業

July 6, 1998

Dear Simon,

Your graduation and rapid acquisition of a job is a cause for congratulations and has inspired us all. To see your hard work and dedication pay off so soon with such a good position must make you and your parents very proud. I wish you the best of luck in your new job and hope you will be successful in your career.

Yours sincerely,

NOTES

1 acquisition 〔,ækwə′zɪʃən〕 n. 獲得
2 **pay off** 可作不同的解釋, 如償還、報仇、收穫等。在這兒是「收穫」的意思, 如 His patience and persistence finally paid off. (他的耐心與毅力終於有了收穫。)

USEFUL EXPRESSIONS

* Wishing you a bright future in your new job.
  祝你事業鴻圖大展。
* Heartfelt congratulations on your graduation and your new career.
  衷心恭喜你畢業展開職業生涯。

Graduation · Employment

1998 年 7 月 6 日

親愛的賽門:

　　恭喜你畢業且迅速就業, 我們大家都非常興奮。眼見你的努力及投入, 能這麼快的由一個好職位獲得回報, 你與父母必定感到光榮萬分。願你新工作一切順利, 並祝你在事業上鴻圖大展。

敬上

 祝賀陞遷

April 1, 1998

Dear Jeff,

We were all overjoyed to hear the news of
your promotion. Your new job is, after all, no
more than you deserve. I am delighted that
you now have received recognition of your tal-
ents and the hard work you have done in the
past. This is something that I think you should
be justly proud of.

I hope your new assignment provides you
with a great deal of excitement and stimulation.
I am looking forward to your telling me all about
your new position and co-workers.

Congratulations again and I hope you will
have more successes in the future.

Yours truly,

Promotion

1998 年 4 月 1 日

親愛的傑夫:

聽到你陞遷的消息,我們都欣喜若狂。畢竟,這個新職位你是當之無愧。如今你的才能與過去的努力均得到肯定,我眞爲你感到高興,我也認爲你應該引以爲傲。

希望你的新工作帶給你許多鼓舞與激勵。我期待聽到有關你新職位與同事方面的細節。

再次恭喜你,也祝你日後步步高升。

敬上

1. recognition〔͵rɛkəg'nɪʃən〕*n.* 讚譽
2. stimulation〔͵stɪmjə'leʃən〕*n.* 激勵
3. co-worker 同事(= *colleague*)

航空郵簡的寫法

航空郵簡（Aerogramme）是信紙與信封合而為一的形式。使用時只需將信文寫在內面，再折疊成信封的樣子，並在正面寫上寄信人與收信人的姓名、地址，即可投遞。航空郵簡重量輕，郵資也較便宜，寄往美加地區的航空郵簡只需十二元，但如寄航空信到美國，至少也要花十五元。航空郵簡內不得放入其他東西，否則會被當作一般信件來處理，結果不是要補繳郵資，就是郵件由水陸寄發。

正式婚禮邀請

Mr. and Mrs. Joseph Clayton

request the honor of your presence

at the marriage of their son

Roger Edward

to

Ms. Audrey Michelle Schmidt

Sunday, August 15th at two o'clock

at Holy Family Catholic Church

Taipei

as well as at the reception, Grand Hyatt

約瑟夫·克雷頓夫婦

敬邀閣下光臨

其子羅傑·愛德華

及

奧黛麗·蜜雪兒·史密特小姐

的結婚典禮

八月十五日星期天二點鐘

天主教聖家堂

台北

並請光臨在凱悅飯店的喜宴

接受婚禮邀請

Mr. and Mrs. Brian Lundberg
accept with pleasure the invitation of
Mr. and Mrs. Joseph Clayton
to the marriage of their son
Roger Edward
to
Ms. Audrey Michelle Schmidt
Sunday, August 15th at two o'clock
at Holy Family Catholic Church
and the reception at the Grand Hyatt

布萊恩・藍伯夫婦
榮幸接受
約瑟夫・克雷頓夫婦邀請
參加其子羅傑・愛德華
與
奧黛麗・蜜雪兒・史密特小姐
之結婚典禮
八月十五日星期天兩點鐘
天主教聖家堂
及凱悅飯店的喜宴

謝絕婚禮邀請

Mr. and Mrs. Brian Lundberg regret that they will not be able to attend the wedding of Mr. and Mrs. Joseph Clayton's son, Roger Edward on Sunday, August 15th or the wedding reception afterwards.

布萊恩·藍伯夫婦，遺憾無法參加八月十五日星期天，約瑟夫·克雷頓夫婦之子，羅傑·愛德華的婚禮，以及婚禮後的喜宴。

** reception〔rɪˈsɛpʃən〕 *n.* 酒會

非正式婚禮邀請

May 1, 1998

Dear Jane,

　　Anna and I are getting married this Saturday at Saint Mary's, around 11 a.m. I hope you will be able to be there as well as stop by our new place for the reception. Please let us know if you can come as soon as possible.

Affectionately,

1998年5月1日

親愛的珍：

　　安娜與我將於本週六的十一點左右，在聖瑪麗教堂舉行婚禮。我希望妳能到場，並順便光臨我們的新房，接受設宴款待。請儘快給我回音。

上

** _stop by_ 稍作停留

接受婚禮邀請

May 2, 1998

Dear Mark,

Of course I will come to your wedding.
You won't be able to keep me and Jenny away.
I will see you around 10 : 30 Saturday.

Your friend,

〰〰〰〰〰〰〰

1998年5月2日

親愛的馬克：

　　我當然會去參加你的婚禮，我和珍妮是你趕也趕不走的。禮拜六的十點半見。

友

** *keep away* 使遠離

謝絕婚禮邀請

May 2, 1998

Dear Cathy,

I am sorry to say that David and I can't make it to your wedding next month. Unfortunately we have a prior engagement. It is very bad timing for all of us because we both really wanted to be there.

Anyway I hope you'll have a wonderful wedding in spite of us not being able to attend and I hope to get in touch with you after your honeymoon.

Your friend,

Declining an Invitation

1998 年 5 月 2 日

親愛的凱西：

　　我很遺憾，大衞和我下個月無法去參加你的婚禮。很不巧地，我們已有別的安排。時間眞是不配合，因爲我們倆都非常想去觀禮。

　　無論如何，雖然我們無法參加，我還是祝福你有個美好的婚禮，也希望在你度完蜜月後能再聯絡。

友

NOTES

1 prior〔ˈpraɪɚ〕*adj.* 之前的

2 in spite of ＝ despite 儘管

3 *get in touch with sb.* 與某人聯絡

4 engagement〔ɪnˈgedʒmənt〕*n.* 預約

INFORMATION

據說從前在斯堪地那維亞（Scandinavia）或英國的婚宴上，大家會飲用蜜作的蜜酒（mead），而新婚夫婦在第一個月也有飲用這種酒的習慣，moon 亦有「月」（month）的意思，所以新婚的第一個月便稱作 honeymoon 了。但亦有一種說法：honeymoon 暗示新婚夫婦的愛很容易產生變化，就像有盈有虧的月亮。

正式晚宴邀請

Mr. and Mrs. Brad Wilkinson

would like for you to attend

a dinner party

Sunday, March 30th

at seven thirty

100 Tienmu East Road Taipei

R.S.V.P.

布雷德‧維京森夫婦

邀您參加

晚宴

三月三十日星期天

七點半

台北天母東路 100 號

謹候回覆

➡ **R.S.V.P.** 是法文 Repondez sil vous plait 的縮寫，意爲敬請
回覆（Reply if you please），亦可寫作 **RSVP** 或 **rsvp**。

接受晚宴邀請

Mr. and Mrs. William Grant

accept the invitation of

Mr. and Mrs. Brad Wilkinson

to a dinner party

Sunday, March 30th at 7:30

100 Tienmu East Road Taipei

威廉・葛蘭特夫婦

接受

布雷德・維京森夫婦

晚宴邀請

三月三十日星期天 7:30

台北天母東路 100 號

謝絕晚宴邀請

　　Mr. and Mrs. William Grant are flattered by the invitation of Mr. and Mrs. Brad Wilkinson to dine on Sunday, March 30th, however they regret that they will not be able to attend, due to a previous engagement.

　　威廉·葛蘭特夫婦，感謝布雷德·維京森夫婦，三月三十日星期天的晚宴之邀，但因有約在身，遺憾無法參加。

**　flatter〔'flætɚ〕 v. 使高興
　　due to 由於
　　previous〔'prɪvɪəs〕 adj. 先前的

非正式晚宴邀請

April 4, 1998

Dear Brian,

This Friday evening Charles and I are planning to have a small dinner party and we would like for you to come.

It's not going to be a formal dinner, so just come as you are, around nine.

Your friend,

1998年4月4日

親愛的布萊恩：

本週五晚上，查理和我打算舉辦一個小型的晚宴，我們希望你能賞光。

那不是正式的晚宴，請在九點左右來，人到就好。

友

接受晚宴邀請

April 5, 1998

Dear Dan,

We would be delighted to come to dinner on Friday, it is nice of you to invite us. Don't worry, we'll be there at nine. If you need anything or would like some help, please do let us know.

Affectionately,

1998年4月5日

親愛的丹：

　　謝謝你的邀請，我們禮拜五將樂意前赴你的晚宴。不用擔心，我們會準時九點到。如果你需要任何東西或幫忙，請務必告訴我們。

上

謝絕晚宴邀請

April 5, 1998

Dear Faith,

It was very kind of you to invite us around for dinner on Friday but I am afraid we can't possibly make it. Unfortunately we have a prior engagement and we can't break it this late. I am sorry, as we would have loved to have been able to come.

Yours sincerely,

1998年4月5日

親愛的費思：

　　謝謝你週五邀請我們吃晚飯，但是我們恐怕無法赴宴。很不巧地我們已有別的約會，無法這麼晚再變卦。我很遺憾，因為我們真的希望能夠前往。

敬上

邀請朋友來訪

August 17, 1998

Dear George,

As we haven't seen each other for a while, how would you like to come to our country home and spend the weekend with us? We would love to see you and you'll enjoy the fresh air.

Do let us know as soon as possible.

Your friend,

1998 年 8 月 17 日

親愛的喬治：

我們已有好一陣子不見了，你想不想到我們鄉下老家來，與我們共度週末？我們很想見你，你也可以享受一下新鮮的空氣。

請儘早給我們回音。

友

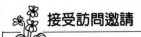 **接受訪問邀請**

August 20, 1998

Dear Keith,

We would be very happy to come and visit you this weekend. We will come by at about six thirty this Friday evening, traffic permitting. I have my golf clubs ready. Do send my love to your wife, and I'll see you on Friday.

Yours,

1998 年 8 月 20 日

親愛的吉斯：

　　我們非常樂意於週末前去做客。如果交通順暢，我們將在週五晚上六點半左右抵達。我已準備好我的高爾夫球桿。請代我向你太太致意，禮拜五見。

上

** club〔klʌb〕 *n.* 棒棍

謝絕訪問邀請

August 20, 1998

Dear Hugh,

I am terribly disappointed at not being able to drop by this weekend, as I have other pressing business in town. Do come in to the office to see me this week, and we will see if we can arrange another date.

Yours,

1998 年 8 月 20 日

親愛的休：

我非常失望這個週末無法到府上拜訪，因為我在城裡有緊急的業務要處理。這星期記得來我的辦公室，我們來研究看看是否可約改天。

上

** pressing〔ˈprɛsɪŋ〕*adj.* 急迫的

延期邀請（正式）

It is with regret that Mr. and Mrs. Ma are unable to attend dinner on Monday the twenty sixth of November at the Grand Hotel, and are forced to postpone this event until the twelfth of December, at eight thirty.

❊❊❊❊❊❊❊❊❊❊❊❊❊

馬先生夫婦很遺憾，無法參加十一月廿六日星期一圓山大飯店的晚宴，不得已要延到十二月十二日八點三十分。

❀ Party 總滙

party in honor of a teacher 謝師宴
New Year's dinner party 新年餐會
birthday party 生日宴會　welcoming party 歡迎酒會
farewell party 惜別酒會　wedding party 結婚喜宴
anniversary party 週年宴　Christmas party 聖誕派對
dinner party 正式晚宴　garden party 園遊會
cocktail party 雞尾酒會　picnic party 野餐會
stag party 男士的餐會　housewarming party 喬遷宴
bachelor's party 單身漢惜別會（為準新郎 groom-to-be 所舉辦的；為準新娘 bride-to-be 舉辦的單身惜別會稱為 bridal shower。）

延期邀請(非正式)

July 27, 1998

Dear Jennifer,

Due to some last minute problems with the work schedule, I am afraid that that dinner next Thursday is impossible.　It has now been postponed until next Friday, at nine thirty.　I am sorry for the trouble and hope you can come on the revised date.

Yours truly,

1998 年 7 月 27 日

親愛的珍妮佛：

　　由於工作進度在最後關頭發生的一些問題，我想下週四的晚餐恐怕無法如期舉行，現在已延到下週五的九點半。很抱歉給妳添麻煩，希望換個時間後，妳還是能夠賞光。

敬上

** postpone〔ˌpostˈpon〕v. 延緩

取消邀請（正式）

It is regretable that due to the unfortunate death of a close relative, Dr. and Mrs. Chang have to cancel their invitation for dinner on Thursday the second of March.

很抱歉由於一位近親不幸逝世，張博士夫婦必須取消他們三月二號星期四的晚宴邀請。

取消邀請(非正式)

August 15, 1998

Dear Leah,

As I am sure you have heard, our eldest boy John has been in an accident and is now in the hospital.

Naturally there is no question of our going forward with our plans for next week. I am sorry for the trouble you have gone to, but I hope you will understand.

I look forward to hearing from you.

Your friend,

Canceling an Invitation

1998 年 8 月 15 日

親愛的利亞：

　　相信你一定已經聽說，我們的大兒子約翰出了事情，現在人躺在醫院裡。

　　自然我們已無心進行下週的計劃。很抱歉給你添麻煩，但是我希望你能諒解。

　　期盼收到你的來信。

友

** ***there is no question of*** 不可能
　　go forward 進展
　　look forward to 期盼　to 為介系詞, 後面須加動名詞
　　hear from sb. 收到某人的信件或電話

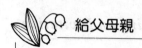

November 5, 1998

Dear Mom and Dad,

I would like to apologize for my letter being so late, as things have been hectic in the office.

I read your latest letter with enjoyment. I am always pleased to hear from you and delighted you are both so well. I have not been in touch with many of my relatives back home lately so your news was especially appreciated.

Nothing very special has happened to me since my last letter. I'm still happy with my new job and I think the work suits me.

Although my work commitments are pressing, I will be sure to make it back home this New Year's Day. I will write with the details later. Please give all my love to everyone and tell them I will see them soon.

Your affectionate son,

NOTES

1 hectic 〔'hɛktɪk〕 adj. 忙碌的
2 commitment 〔kə'mɪtmənt〕 n.
任務

USEFUL EXPRESSIONS

請人代爲問候可用 *Please remember me to ~* . 或 *Please give my best regards to ~* . (用於長輩。)

To Parents

1998 年 11 月 5 日

親愛的爸媽：

　　抱歉這麼遲才寫信給你們，實在是辦公室裏太忙了。

　　讀了你們上回的來信，我覺得好快樂。收到你們的來信，知道你們一切安好，總讓我感到高興與欣慰。近來我和家鄉的許多親戚都沒聯絡，因此特別感謝你們告訴我一些消息。

　　自我上封信後，沒發生什麼特別的事。我仍工作愉快，我覺得這工作挺適合我的。

　　雖然我的工作緊迫，我一定會趕在過年時回家。至於細節，我以後再談。請代我向大家問好，也請告訴他們，我很快便能與大家見面。

兒子　敬上

給兄弟姊妹

November 11, 1998

Dear Sam,

I was surprised to have heard from you so soon. The news about your job was really exciting. I am very pleased for you.

Mom also wrote me about your new girlfriend. If it is serious, let me know and I'll come back. I am sure the only thing Mom would like to hear more than the sound of wedding bells is the patter of little feet!

It seems so long since we saw each other. I'll try to come home this holiday season. We have a great deal of catching up to do. I look forward to seeing you then.

Give my love to everyone, I miss them all, and write soon.

Your brother,

To a Sibling

1998 年 11 月 11 日

親愛的山姆：

　　沒想到這麼快就收到你的信。關於你工作的消息，眞是令人興奮，我眞爲你高興。

　　媽也寫信告訴我你新女朋友的事。如果你是認眞的話，就讓我知道，我會回來。我相信，唯一比婚禮的鐘聲，更讓媽期盼的，莫過於小孩的腳步聲。

　　我們好久不見了，這個長假我會想辦法回家一趟。我們有好多未完的事要做，期待到時候見。

　　代我向大家問候，我想念每一個人，請快回信。

兄

＊＊ patter〔'pætɚ〕**n.** 急速的輕拍聲
catch up 彌補落後

 **給親戚**

September 20, 1998

Dear Alex and Jo,

It has been a long time since we had a good talk. So I will write about what I have been doing recently.

I have been fine. I like my new job and have settled in very well. My colleagues are all considerate and supportive, so it has been easy to adapt. Living so far from my family is another matter. Taking care of myself is certainly harder than I expected and of course the food is not as good, so the next time I see you I hope you will cook all your best dishes. I'm looking forward to it.

The weather these last few weeks has been fairly cold, so your gift is useful. I wear it as often as possible and think of you both when I put it on, thanks.

Do tell me what you have been doing. I miss you both and am eager for any news. I hope you are well.

Your nephew,

To Relatives

1998 年 9 月 20 日

親愛的亞歷士和喬：

　　我們已許久不曾好好聊聊了，所以我來報告一下我的近況。

　　我最近很好，我喜歡我的新工作，並且適應良好。我的同事都很善體人意，且樂於助人，所以很容易就進入軌道。至於離鄉背井就另當別論了。照顧自己的確比我想像的要難，而且伙食當然也比不上家裏的好。所以下次再見面時，我希望能嚐遍你們的拿手好菜。我真是等不及了。

　　這幾個禮拜來，天氣非常寒冷，所以你們的禮物派上了用場。我常穿它，當我套上衣服時，總會想起你們，謝謝。

　　請務必告訴我你們的近況。我非常思念您倆位，熱切盼望獲得你們的音訊。祝你們身體健康。

姪兒

INFORMATION ···············

　　外國人的親戚稱謂不像中國人的複雜，對於叔伯、舅舅、姑丈、姨丈都稱作 uncle，伯母、嬸嬸、姑媽、姨媽則稱 aunt。nephew 是姪子或外甥，而 niece 是姪女、外甥女。對於 uncle 或 aunt 的子女稱呼 cousin。

給師長

September 20, 1998

Dear Mr. Fisher,

I hope you have been well in the years since I saw you last. Graduation does not seem that long ago to me and the memory of your lectures is with me still.

I would like to thank you again for your warm recommendation. I believe it was largely through your personal evaluation that I was given my position. I really can't thank you enough. I am sure you'll be glad to hear that I'll be up for promotion this fall.

If you have the time to spare, I would appreciate a letter from you about school or my classmates. I am afraid that we've been out of touch.

I wish you the best of health and remain

Your respectful student,

To a Teacher

1998 年 9 月 20 日

親愛的費雪老師：

　　希望自我上次見過您後，這些年來您一切安好。畢業彷彿才是不久前的事，我依舊記得您上課的情景。

　　再次感謝您熱心的推薦，我深信，正因您素富聲望，我才能獲得今日的職位。我對您實在感激不盡。相信您會很高興聽到，我秋天時就會升職了。

　　倘若您有空，我會很感謝您能來函，告訴我有關學校與同學們的消息，很遺憾的，我們已經失去聯繫了。

　　祝您身體健康

永遠尊敬您的學生

** recommendation〔͵rɛkəmɛnˈdeʃən〕*n.* 推薦
out of touch 失去聯絡；*keep in touch* 保持聯絡

給朋友

March 3, 1998

Dear Sean,

I was just thinking of home yesterday when I realized I haven't written to you; sorry about that. How have you been? I heard you were looking for a new job. How is it going? I can't believe you stayed at that old company for so long. Do you remember us both driving there for the interview?

Things here are pretty much the same. I am working hard but looking forward to dropping in on you one day soon.

Do you remember Steve? He is getting married. Will you be going to the wedding? If so, let me know. We'll get together and go out like we did at school. Got to cut this short. Write to me and tell me how things are going soon.

Your best friend,

To a Friend

1998 年 3 月 3 日

親愛的史恩：

　　我昨天在想家時，才發現我還没寫信給你，眞是抱歉。你近來好嗎？我聽說你在找新工作，進行得如何？我不敢相信你在原來那家公司待了這麼久。你還記得我們倆一道開車去那兒面試嗎？

　　這兒一切都還是老樣子。我工作得非常賣力，但還是希望能儘快找個時間，順道拜訪你。

　　你還記得史蒂夫嗎？他要結婚了。你會去參加婚禮嗎？如果會的話，請跟我說一聲。我們可以像從前學生時一樣，聚在一起一塊出去玩。不多說了，早日寫信給我告知近況。

好友

** *drop in on sb*. 順道拜訪某人

 給筆友

October 12, 1998

Dear Mary,

　　Thank you for your prompt reply.　It was a pleasure to read your letter and I was fascinated by your account of life in Ireland.

　　Since I told you all about my family, little has changed.　My brother did well on a test, so he and my mother are proud.　My dog was slightly ill but he is fine now.

　　Recently in Taiwan we have had the Double Ten holiday.　It was a celebration with parades and fireworks.　It was very grand. Do you have anything like that in Ireland?

　　I hope to hear from you soon and to hear more about life in Ireland.

　　　　　　　　　　　　　　　Your pen pal,

NOTES

1 prompt〔prɑmpt〕*adj*. 迅速的
2 parade〔pə'red〕*n*. 遊行
3 fireworks〔'faɪr,wɜks〕*n*. 煙火
   firecracker〔'faɪr,krækɚ〕*n*. 爆竹

USEFUL EXPRESSIONS

愛爾蘭國際筆友會（I.P.F.）在全世界擁有 300,000 名會員，是尋找筆友的好管道，有興趣者可向該會詢問，地址是台南郵政 9-22 號信箱。

To a Pen Pal

1998 年 10 月 12 日

親愛的瑪麗：

　　謝謝你這麼快就回信。讀妳的信真是愉快，我被妳所描述的愛爾蘭生活給迷住了。

　　自我告訴妳家人的近況後，幾乎沒什麼變化。我弟弟考得不錯，媽媽和他都引以爲傲。我的小狗有點不舒服，不過牠現在已痊癒了。

　　最近台灣在慶祝雙十節，慶典有遊行還有煙火，實在很壯觀。你們愛爾蘭有類似的活動嗎？

　　我盼望能快點收到你的信，也希望多聽到一些愛爾蘭的生活。

筆友

美國各州州名（一）

州		名	縮	寫
英 文		中 文	舊 式	新 式
Alabama〔͵ælə'bæmə〕		阿 拉 巴 馬	Ala.	A L
Alaska〔ə'læskə〕		阿 拉 斯 加	Alas.	A K
Arizona〔͵ærə'zonə〕		亞 利 桑 納	Ariz.	A Z
Arkansas〔'ɑrkən͵sɔ〕		阿 肯 色	Ark.	A R
California〔͵kælə'fɔrnɪə〕		加利福尼亞	Calif.	C A
Colorado〔͵kɑlə'rɑdo〕		科 羅 拉 多	Colo.	C O
Connecticut〔kə'nɛtɪkət〕		康 乃 狄 克	Conn.	C T
Delaware〔'dɛlə͵wɛr〕		達 拉 威	Del.	D E
District of Columbia〔͵dɪstrɪkt əv kə'lʌmbɪə〕		哥倫比亞特區	D.C.	D C
Florida〔'flɔrədə〕		佛 羅 里 達	Fla.	F L
Georgia〔'dʒɔrdʒə〕		喬 治 亞	Ga.	G A
Hawaii〔hə'waɪ·i〕		夏 威 夷	H.I.	H I
Idaho〔'aɪdə͵ho〕		愛 達 荷	Ida.	I D
Illinois〔͵ɪlə'nɔɪz〕		伊 利 諾	Ill.	I L
Indiana〔͵ɪndɪ'ænə〕		印 地 安 那	Ind.	I N
Iowa〔'aɪəwə〕		愛 荷 華	Ia.	I A
Kansas〔'kænzəs〕		堪 薩 斯	Kans.	K S
Kentucky〔kən'tʌkɪ〕		肯 塔 基	Ky.	K Y
Louisiana〔͵lʊɪzɪ'ænə〕		路易西安那	La.	L A
Maine〔men〕		緬 因	Me.	M E
Maryland〔'mɛrɪlənd〕		馬 里 蘭	Md.	M D
Massachusetts〔͵mæsə'tʃusɪts〕		麻 薩 諸 塞	Mass.	M A
Michigan〔'mɪʃəgən〕		密 西 根	Mich.	M I
Minnesota〔͵mɪnɪ'sotə〕		明 尼 蘇 達	Minn.	M N
Mississippi〔͵mɪsə'sɪpɪ〕		密 西 西 比	Miss.	M S

婚禮通知

October 1, 1998

Dear John,

I have some very surprising news for you.
I finally asked Anna to marry me and she said
yes! As you know we have been together for a
long time and we decided now was the right time.

I hope you will be coming to the wedding
next Sunday at Saint Mary's, around 11 A.M.
and that you will write to me to let me know.

Your friend,

1998 年 10 月 1 日

親愛的約翰：

我有個驚人的消息要告訴你。我終於向安娜求婚，
而她答應了！你知道我們在一起很久了，我們決定現
在正是結婚的時候。

我希望你能參加下星期天上午十一點，在聖瑪麗
教堂的婚禮，請給我回音。

友

死訊通知

February 10, 1998

Dear Mrs. Smith,

It is with deep sorrow that I must inform you that my father passed away last night. As a long term friend and colleague, I am sure it will come as some small comfort that, despite his long illness, his final hours were peaceful and comfortable.

The funeral will be held at St. Mary's on February 15, around 10 a.m. The burial will be at Chinshan cemetery immediately after the service.

Yours sincerely,

Passing Away

1998 年 2 月 10 日

親愛的史密斯夫人：

　　很難過必須通知您，家父於昨晚過世了。您是他多年的朋友兼同事，我相信您會稍感寬慰得知，雖然家父久病在身，他臨終前却是平靜而安詳。

　　葬禮將在二月十五日上午十點左右，於聖瑪麗教堂舉行。葬禮過後隨即埋於青山墓地。

敬上

** ***pass away*** 去世　　　funeral〔ˈfjunərəl〕*n.* 葬禮
　　burial〔ˈbɛrɪəl〕*n.* 埋葬
　　cemetery〔ˈsɛmə,tɛrɪ〕*n.* 墓地

通知嬰兒誕生

January 24, 1998

Dear Nora,

I would like to inform you that Cindy delivered a baby boy last night at National Taiwan University Hospital. The baby weighed two and a half kilograms and both he and his mother are doing well. Which name is better for him, Steven or Scott?

Your brother,

1998 年 1 月 24 日

親愛的諾拉：

我要告訴你，辛蒂昨晚在台大醫院生下一男孩。嬰兒重兩千五百公克，母子皆平安。哪個名字比較適合他？史蒂夫還是史考特？

兄

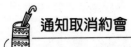 通知取消約會

June 13, 1998

Dear Dr. Yang,

Due to pressing business in Taiwan, I am afraid I will not be able to keep my appointment for next Tuesday. I regret any inconvenience this may cause and I hope it will be possible to arrange another appointment for next Wednesday. I'll ring you on Friday to confirm the details.

Yours sincerely,

1998 年 6 月 13 日

親愛的楊博士：

由於台灣的業務緊迫，我下週二恐怕無法赴約。我對可能引起的不便深感抱歉，同時我也希望，若有可能的話，能於下週三再安排另一次見面。我會於週五打電話給你以敲定細節。

敬上

搬家通知

December 12, 1998

Dear Sean,

I have finally moved out of the old house. My new address is below, so don't write to the old one anymore.

Do drop in whenever you're passing by, I am looking forward to hearing from you.

Affectionately yours,

1998 年 12 月 12 日

親愛的史恩：

我終於搬離了舊家。我的新地址如下，所以不要再寫信到舊地址了。

你路過的時候，一定要順道來看我，我也期待著你的來信。

上

** *drop in* 順道拜訪

通知變更地址

November 23, 1998

Dear Sir,

This is to inform you of a change in my address. I am no longer living at 108 Hoping East Road, Section 3 but am now on the eleventh floor of 57 Chung Shan North Road Section 3, Taipei, Taiwan 10305 Republic of China. I would appreciate all further deliveries be made to this new address.

Yours sincerely,

1998 年 11 月 23 日

敬啟者：

特此通知您我的地址有所變更。我已不住在和平東路三段 108 號，我的現址是中華民國台灣省台北市中山北路三段 57 號 11 樓，郵遞區號 10305。麻煩今後所有的郵件都送到這個新址。

敬上

美國各州州名（二）

州	名		縮	寫
英　　　　　　　　文	中　　　文	舊　式	新　式
Missouri〔mə'zʊrɪ〕	密　蘇　里	Mo.	MO
Montana〔mɑn'tænə〕	蒙　大　拿	Mont.	MT
Nebraska〔nə'bræskə〕	內布拉斯加	Nebr.	NB
Nevada〔nə'vædə〕	內　華　達	Nev.	NV
New Hampshire〔nju'hæmpʃɪr〕	新罕布夏	N.H.	NH
New Jersey〔nju'dʒɝzɪ〕	新　澤　西	N.J.	NJ
New Mexico〔nju'mɛksɪ,ko〕	新墨西哥	N.M.	NM
New York〔nju'jɔrk〕	紐　　　約	N.Y.	NY
North Carolina〔nɔrθ,kærə'laɪnə〕	北卡羅來納	N.C.	NC
North Dakota〔nɔrθ,də'kotə〕	北達科塔	N.D.	ND
Ohio〔o'haɪo〕	俄亥俄	O.	OH
Oklahoma〔,oklə'homə〕	奧克拉荷馬	Okla.	OK
Oregon〔'arɪ,gɑn〕	俄勒岡	Oreg.	OR
Pennsylvania〔pɛnsḷ'venjə〕	賓夕凡尼亞	Pa.	PA
Rhode Island〔rod'aɪlənd〕	羅德島	R.I.	RI
South Carolina〔sauθ,kærə'laɪnə〕	南卡羅來納	S.C.	SC
South Dakota〔sauθ,də'kotə〕	南達科塔	S.D.	SD
Tennessee〔'tɛnə,si〕	田納西	Tenn.	TN
Texas〔'tɛksəs〕	德克薩斯	Tex.	TX
Utah〔'juta〕	猶　　　他	Utah	UT
Vermont〔və'mɑnt〕	佛蒙特	Vt.	VT
Virginia〔və'dʒɪnjə〕	維吉尼亞	Va.	VA
Washington〔'waʃɪŋtən〕	華　盛　頓	Wash.	WA
West Virginia〔wɛst,və'dʒɪnjə〕	西維吉尼亞	W.Va.	WV
Wisconsin〔wɪs'kɑnsṇ〕	威斯康辛	Wis.	WI
Wyoming〔'waɪəmɪŋ〕	懷俄明	Wyo.	WY

慰問生病

February 5, 1998

Dear Mrs. Jones,

I am very sorry to hear that you are not feeling well. Everyone here misses you and hopes you will be on your feet again soon. Wishing you a speedy recovery.

Yours,

1998 年 2 月 5 日

親愛的瓊斯太太：

聽說你生病的消息，我感到很難過。這兒的每一個人都念著妳，都盼望妳會很快好起來。祝妳儘速康復。

上

疾病名稱

allergy〔'æləʤɪ〕過敏症

influenza〔,ɪnflʊ'ɛnzə〕流行性感冒

hepatitis〔,hɛpə'taɪtɪs〕肝炎

diabetes〔,daɪə'bitɪs〕糖尿病

chicken pox 水痘

pneumonia〔nju'monjə〕肺炎

asthma〔'æsmə〕氣喘

fracture〔'fræktʃə〕骨折

hypertension〔,haɪpə'tɛnʃən〕高血壓

stomach ulcer〔'stʌmək'ʌlsə〕胃潰瘍

慰問災難

July 7, 1998

Dear Mark,

I just heard the awful news of the terrible calamity. We are all worried about you, so I thought I would drop you a line as soon as possible.

If there is anything you need or anything we can do, please don't hesitate to let us know. Any news of you and your family would set our minds at ease. We are all praying for you.

Yours sincerely,

NOTES

1 calamity [kə'læmətɪ] n. 災難
2 hesitate ['hɛzə,tet] v. 不願

USEFUL EXPRESSIONS

* I was numb with shock after reading this morning's paper that your house had been gutted by a fire last night. 讀了今早的報紙，知道你們家慘遭祝融之災，我實在震驚不已。

Calamities

1998 年 7 月 7 日

親愛的馬克：

　　我剛聽說了那件可怕的不幸事件。我們都非常擔心你，所以我才想要儘快寫封信給你。

　　如果你有什麼需要，或有我們能效勞的地方，請務必告訴我們。請捎來你及你家人的音訊，好讓我們放心。我們都在爲你祈禱。

上

慰問落榜

July 5, 1998

Dear Matthew,

It was sad to see that you did not do as well as expected in the examination. We all feel sympathy for you. At this time the most important thing is not to be discouraged. If at first you don't succeed, try, try again. With the determination I know you have, I do not doubt that at this time next year you will pass with flying colors.

Your friend,

1998 年 7 月 5 日

親愛的馬修:

很遺憾得知你考試結果,未如預期理想,我們都為你感到難過。此刻最重要的,就是不要灰心,如果一開始沒有成功,就該再接再厲。抱持你的決心,我深信明年此時,你會順利地通過考試。

友

** determination 〔dɪ͵tɝməˈneʃən〕 *n.* 決心

慰問失業

December 12, 1998

Dear Sam,

The news of your dismissal was a great surprise to me and many of your other friends. I hope you will not take it too hard, there are plenty of employers out there looking for talented workers and I am sure you will find a new position soon. In the meantime if you need any help or assistance, let me know as soon as possible.

Your friend,

1998 年 12 月 12 日

親愛的山姆：

你被解聘的消息傳來，令我及其他的朋友都很意外。希望你不要看得太嚴重，有許多僱主在尋找優秀的員工，我相信你很快就能謀得新職。在這段期間，若你需要任何協助，請儘快讓我知道。

友

** dismissal〔dɪsˈmɪsl〕 *n.* 解僱

慰問失戀

June 6, 1998

Dear Henry,

While you must be devastated by your recent breakup, I would like to offer a few words of consolation.

Everyone must have at some time had a disappointing relationship. The important thing is that you do not despair. Remember that there are plenty of fish in the sea and if the two of you were not meant to be together, it is better to know sooner than later.

While now my words must ring hollow, please remember time heals all wounds and that one day you will find someone better.

Yours sincerely,

Breakup

1998 年 6 月 6 日

親愛的亨利：

　　在你最近與女友分手、整個人消沈之際，我有幾句話想說，希望能撫慰你的心靈。

　　每個人在一生中，總會有一段失意的感情，重要的是你不能因而絕望。天涯何處無芳草，若你倆不是注定的一對，還不如早點覺悟。

　　雖然我的話現在聽起來一定很空洞，請記住時間會治療一切創傷。總有一天，你會找到更理想的對象。

敬上

NOTES

1. devastate〔ˋdɛvəstet〕*v.* 摧殘
2. ***breakup*** 作名詞，是「分手，絕交」的意思。也可將它拆開，變成動詞片語，如 I broke up with her.(我和她吹了。)
3. there are plenty of fish in the sea 或 there are other fish in the ocean 都是用來安慰情場失意的人，指機會眾多，一定可以找到適合的對象。
4. hollow〔ˋhɑlo〕*adj.* 空洞

USEFUL EXPRESSIONS

* If two hearts are to be united, they must beat as one.
  兩心若要相印，必須和諧一致。
* Though painful, the end of a relationship is a common thing.
  雖然痛苦，失戀卻如家常便飯。
* The sooner it ends, the happier both will be.
  愈早結束，彼此都會快樂。

國內函件郵資表

單位：新臺幣元

信　函　類　別		計　　費　　標　　準	
信　　函 （每件限重不逾二公斤）	普通	不逾 20 公克	5.00
		逾 20 公克至 50 公克	10.00
		逾 50 公克至 100 公克	15.00
		逾 100 公克至 250 公克	25.00
	限時	不逾 20 公克	12.00
		逾 20 公克至 50 公克	17.00
		逾 50 公克至 100 公克	22.00
		逾 100 公克至 250 公克	32.00
印　刷　物	普通	不逾 50 公克	3.50
		逾 50 公克至 100 公克	7.50
		逾 100 公克至 250 公克	10.00
	限時	不逾 50 公克	10.50
		逾 50 公克至 100 公克	14.50
		逾 100 公克至 250 公克	17.00
明　信　片	普通	每　件	2.50
	限時	每　件	9.50
小　　包 （每件限重不逾一公斤）		每重 100 公克	10.00
備 註	限時專送費：7.00　　　掛號費：14.00　　　回執費：9.00 航空費：每重 20 公克另加 2 元		

資料來源：交通部郵政總局，八十二年六月一日起實施。
　　　　　資料若有變更，請逕向有關單位查詢。

一般弔唁函

August 3, 1998

Dear Penny,

I was grieved to hear the terrible news. While nothing can make up for your loss, I would like to extend my sympathy from the bottom of my heart. If there is anything you need or anything that I can do, please let me know. You can rely on my full support.

Yours sincerely,

1998年8月3日

親愛的潘妮：

聽到這悲慘的消息，我感到十分傷心。雖然妳的損失無法彌補，我仍衷心致上我的關懷。如果妳有任何需要，或有任何事我能為你效勞，請讓我知道。妳可以仰賴我全力的協助。

敬上

** *make up for* 補償

 弔唁喪親

November 12, 1998

Dear John,

I was saddened to hear the news of your loss. The death of a father is a great blow to anyone. Your father was a man who brought happiness into the lives of many. His legacy consists of the thousands of warm memories he left to those who knew him.

At this tragic moment in your life, I assure you that you can count on my support, should you require it. I extend my most sincere condolences and I am sorry that I can do so little to ease your burden.

Yours sincerely,

NOTES

1. legacy〔'lɛgəsɪ〕*n.* 遺產
2. consist of 包含(= be composed of = contain)
3. condolence〔kən'doləns〕*n.* 哀悼 多用複數形
4. count on 依賴(= rely on = depend on)
5. assure〔ə'ʃʊr〕*v.* 保證
6. burden〔'bɝdn̩〕*n.* 負擔

USEFUL EXPRESSIONS

* Few people are as lucky as you to have a father who is so respected by everyone.
  極少人像你一樣,有個備受尊崇的父親。

* At dark moments like this we will stand by you. 在這悲傷的時刻,我們都支持你。

* Along with those who knew and admired the deceased, may I offer my sincere sympathy. 謹同逝者的友人及仰慕者,致上我誠摯的關懷。

Losing a Parent

1998 年 11 月 12 日

親愛的約翰:

聽到你喪父的消息,我感到很難過。父親的去世,對任何人而言,都是項重大的打擊。你的父親把快樂帶進許多人的生命中,他留給所有認識他的人,萬千溫暖的回憶。

在你生命中這個不幸的時刻,我向你保證,如果有需要的話,你可以仰賴我的援助。致上我最由衷的哀悼之意,也很遺憾我能力微薄,無法減輕你的負擔。

敬上

弔唁喪偶

July 7, 1998

Dear Anne,

The news of the death of your husband David left me heartbroken. The loss of a man with whom you have spent your best years must have come as a great shock. He was a good man, admired by all who knew him.

Please accept my deepest sympathy at this tragic moment and rest assured of the love and support of your friends.

Yours sincerely,

Losing a Spouse

1998 年 7 月 7 日

親愛的安：

　　你丈夫大衛的死訊令我傷心萬分。一個與你共度人生美好時光的人，如今走了，絕對是個沈重的打擊。他是位好人，所有認識他的人都敬愛他。

　　在這悲傷的時刻，請接受我最深切的關懷，也請妳放心，朋友們定會給予關心與協助。

敬上

USEFUL EXPRESSIONS ···············

* I know what you are going through even though I never had an opportunity to know David. 雖然我無緣認識大衛，但我能體會你所受的煎熬。

* In many ways your husband has influenced our lives.
尊夫對我們影響深遠。

* I deeply sympathize with you in your bereavement of your wife. 對你的喪妻之痛，我深表同情。

弔唁喪子

January 10, 1998

Dear Peter and Jane,

I cannot express the sadness I felt when I heard about the death of your son. He was a bright, talented boy who endeared himself to all who met him. His death cut short a young life filled with potential and promise.

As it cannot be easy for you at this moment, I would like to extend my most sincere condolences and sympathy at your loss.

Yours sincerely,

Losing a Child

1998 年 1 月 10 日

親愛的彼得與珍：

　　聽到你喪子的消息，我的哀傷實在難以言喻。他是個聰明伶俐的男孩，見過他的人莫不喜歡。他的去世，中斷了一個充滿前途與希望的生命。

　　在這時刻，你們內心必定不好受。對於你們的損失，我謹致上最誠摯的哀悼與關懷。

敬上

NOTES

[1] *endear oneself to sb.* 使受喜愛

[2] cut short 可指「刪短」或「中斷」，如 cut a long story short（長話短說。）His career was cut short by illness.（他的事業因病中斷。）

[3] potential 〔pə'tɛnʃəl〕 *n.* 前途

[4] promise 〔'pramɪs〕 *n.* 希望

USEFUL EXPRESSIONS

* We are shocked to hear of your great loss. 聞及你的喪痛，我們都為之震驚。

* I share your deep grief after your tragic loss. 你的喪痛，我感同身受。

* Right now it might seem impossible to ever be happy again but remember time heals all wounds. 或許你覺得無法再重拾歡笑，但記得時間會治療一切的創傷。

弔唁喪手足

March 3, 1998

Dear Kathy,

The death of your brother came as a terrible surprise and brought grief to us all. The loss of such a gifted and charitable man is a loss not only to your family but to the whole community. You can rest assured that while his physical presence may have left us bereft, his enduring monument survives all around us in the good works he did.

In this saddest of moments please remember my deepest sympathy for your and his family, and I offer my most heartfelt condolences.

Yours sincerely,

Losing a Sibling

1998年3月3日

親愛的凱西：

　　你弟弟的惡耗傳來，猶如晴天霹靂，帶給我們全體無限哀傷。失去如此有天賦而又樂善好施的人，不僅是你們家的損失，也是整個社會的損失。你可以安心的是，雖然他的形體不能與我們同在，但他永垂不朽的成就，卻於他偉大作品中，長存我們四周。

　　在這最悲慟的時刻，請代我慰問你及他的家人。謹致上我由衷的哀悼之意。

敬上

** charitable〔ˈtʃærətəbḷ〕*adj.* 慈善的
　　bereave〔bəˈriv〕*v.* 剝奪，過去式為
　　bereaved，過去分詞是 bereft。
　　enduring〔ɪnˈdjʊrɪŋ〕*adj.* 不朽的
　　monument〔ˈmɑnjəmənt〕*n.* 永垂不朽之事
　　work 作「藝術作品」解時，常用複數

國際航空函件郵資表

單位：新臺幣元

函件類別	計費標準	香港澳門	亞洲及大洋洲	歐非中南美洲各地	美國加拿大
信　函 （每件限重不逾二公斤）	不逾20公克	9.00			
	每續重20公克	6.00			
	不逾10公克		14.00	18.00	16.00
	每續重10公克		9.00	14.00	13.00
明　信　片	每　　件	6.00	10.00	12.00	11.00
郵　簡	每　　件	8.00	11.00	14.00	12.00
印　刷　物 （每件限重不逾二公斤，書籍及小冊子得展至五公斤）	不逾20公克	7.00	10.00	13.00	13.00
	每續重20公克	5.00	7.00	10.00	10.00
小　包 （每件限重不逾二公斤）	不逾20公克	7.00	10.00	13.00	13.00
	每續重20公克	5.00	7.00	10.00	10.00
備　註	掛號費：除航空資費外每件另加24元，印刷物專袋除航空資費外每袋另加100元。 快遞費：除航空資費外另加30元。				

為犯錯道歉

December 4, 1998

Dear Jane,

I would like to express my regret for my behavior last Saturday. My actions were unwarranted and totally inappropriate. I am very sorry for any embarrassment I may have caused. Mark my words, such an incident will not happen again.

Yours sincerely,

1998 年 12 月 4 日

親愛的珍：

我想要為我上週六的行為道歉。我的舉動不應該且完全不恰當。我為我所可能造成的難堪，深感歉意。請聽我說，這種事情絕不會再發生了。

敬上

**unwarranted〔ʌn'wɔrəntɪd〕*adj.* 不當的

為過失道歉

May 7, 1998

Dear Mr. Brown,

Following the unfortunate incident last week I would like to offer my most sincere apology for the damage done. The fault was entirely mine and I will naturally assume full responsibility for rectifying the situation, financially or otherwise.

I assure you that such behavior on my part will not occur again.

Sincerely yours,

1998 年 5 月 7 日

親愛的布朗先生：

因為上週的不幸事件，我要對我所造成的損害，致上最由衷的歉意。錯全在我，我自然會在財務及其他各方面，全權負起補償的責任。

我向你保證，絕對不會再有這種行為。

敬上

** rectify〔'rɛktə,faɪ〕 v. 改正

為騷擾道歉

November 20, 1998

Dear Mr. and Mrs. King,

It has been brought to our attention that our activities on Friday night caused you some degree of distress. Believe us that this was not our intention and we were unaware of the effect we may have had.

We are very sorry you were disturbed and we assure you that this unfortunate misunderstanding will never occur again.

Yours sincerely,

1998 年 11 月 20 日

親愛的金恩先生及夫人：

我們週五晚上的活動，對你們所造成的一些困擾，已引起我們的關切。請相信這絕非我們的本意，我們當時對可能產生的影響，毫無所覺。

我們非常抱歉打擾到你們，並向你們保證，這樣令人遺憾的誤會絕不會再發生。

敬上

** distress〔dɪ'strɛs〕 n. 困擾

為失約道歉

July 20, 1998

Dear Mr. Jones,

I would like to apologize for missing our agreed meeting yesterday.　I was suddenly taken ill and was unable to get in touch with you before the appointed time. I am sorry for the inconvenience I may have caused you and for my untimely absence.

If there is any later date at which a subsequent meeting could be arranged, I would be most grateful.　I shall contact you later in the week to discuss any possible future arrangement.

Yours sincerely,

Missing an Appointment

1998 年 7 月 20 日

親愛的瓊斯先生：

　　我要爲昨天的失約致歉。我忽然身體不適，又無法及時通知你。對你所可能造成的不便，以及我不當的缺席，我深感抱歉。

　　如果日後能再安排一次會面的話，我會非常感激。我這個禮拜會和你聯絡，以討論是否可能做此安排。

敬上

** *be taken ill* 生病
untimely〔ʌnˈtaɪmlɪ〕*adj.* 不合時機的

➡ 因故失約除道歉外，可請求安排另一次約會。

為取消約會道歉

October 27, 1998

Dear Mr. Smith,

Please accept my apologies for cancelling our appointment on Monday. Unfortunately at the last minute some very urgent business came up. I apologize for wasting your time and I did not mean any disrespect.

If there is any further business that you feel is important, please contact me at your earliest convenience.

Yours sincerely,

Canceling an Appointment

1998 年 10 月 27 日

親愛的史密斯先生：

　　請接受我因取消週一的約會，所致上的歉意。很不巧地，就在我赴約前一刻，發生了非常緊急的事。我很抱歉浪費您寶貴的時間，我絕無意冒犯。

　　如果往後您有任何要務，請您及早撥冗與我聯絡。

敬上

** cancel〔ˈkænsḷ〕*v*. 取消
　urgent〔ˈɝdʒənt〕*adj*. 緊急的
　come up 發生

國際水陸函件郵資表

單位：新臺幣元

函件類別	計　費　標　準	香港澳門	國外其他各地
信　函（每件限重不逾二公斤）	不逾 20 公克	7.00	14.00
	逾　20 公克　不逾 100 公克	17.00	32.00
	逾 100 公克　不逾 250 公克	32.00	65.00
	逾 250 公克　不逾 500 公克	62.00	125.00
	逾 500 公克　不逾 1000 公克	108.00	216.00
	逾 1000 公克　不逾 2000 公克	176.00	352.00
明　信　片	每　件	5.00	9.00
印　刷　物（每件限重不逾二公斤書籍得展至五公斤）	不逾 20 公克	5.00	9.00
	逾　20 公克　不逾 100 公克	10.00	21.00
	逾 100 公克　不逾 250 公克	20.00	38.00
	逾 250 公克　不逾 500 公克	35.00	69.00
	逾 500 公克　不逾 1000 公克	57.00	114.00
	逾 1000 公克　不逾 2000 公克	81.00	160.00
	每續重 1000 公克	40.00	80.00
小　包	不逾 100 公克	10.00	21.00
	逾 100 公克　不逾 250 公克	20.00	38.00
	逾 250 公克　不逾 500 公克	35.00	69.00
	逾 500 公克　不逾 1000 公克	57.00	114.00
	逾 1000 公克　不逾 2000 公克	81.00	160.00
備　註	掛號費：除水陸資費外每件另加 24 元，印刷物專袋除水陸資費外每袋另加 100 元。 快遞費：除水陸資費外每件另加 30 元。 回執費：18.00 元。		

 **感謝幫忙**

November 14, 1998

Dear Sir,

I would like to thank you for your assistance, and the interest you had in my situation. I am pleased to tell you that through your help I finally succeeded and that without your recommendation the issue would have been in doubt.

I will do my best to repay you and I will not let you down.

Yours respectfully,

1998 年 11 月 14 日

親愛的老師：

我要感謝您的協助，及您對我的處境所給予的關心。我很高興能告訴您，由於您的幫助，我終於成功了。若沒有您的忠告，結果可能還在未定中。

我會竭盡所能來回報您，不令您失望。

敬上

** ***let sb. down*** 讓某人失望

 感謝款待

August 3, 1998

Dear Mr. and Mrs. Smith,

I would like to thank you both for a delightful evening the night before last. It was a pleasure to see the two of you again and the dinner was delicious. I am indebted to you for all the trouble caused. It was an evening we shall remember forever.

Yours sincerely,

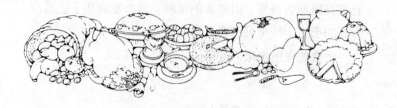

Hospitality

1998 年 8 月 3 日

親愛的史密斯先生及夫人：

　　謝謝賢伉儷前晚招待我，度過了一個愉快的晚上。再度見到二位眞是令人高興，晚餐也非常美味豐盛。多有打擾，我十分過意不去，不過那眞是一個令人難忘的夜晚。

敬上

USEFUL EXPRESSIONS ··············

* Thank you so much for your kind invitation and I hope I'll see you again. 謝謝你們盛情款待，希望能再度見面。
* Last Sunday was a wonderful evening with more fun than we have had in years. 這幾年來，我們不曾像上週日，玩得如此盡興。
* For the most delicious lunch we had in your beautiful garden, let me thank you again. 再次謝謝你在美麗的花園裏所設的豐盛午宴。

感謝慰問

April 5, 1998

Dear Susanna,

Your message reached me at just the right time. Your sympathy and understanding were of great help to me at a very serious moment. Your warm support and offers of help were of much benefit to me.

Thank you very much for being helpful at such a time of need.

Affectionately yours,

1998 年 4 月 5 日

親愛的蘇珊娜：

妳的問候來得正是時候。在這沈重的時刻，妳的關懷與瞭解，對我來說，有莫大的幫助。妳熱心的支持與協助，更讓我獲益良多。

謝謝妳在我需要的時候鼎力相助。

上

感謝贈禮

September 24, 1998

Dear Anna,

   Thank you for your wonderful present. Such a beautiful and charming gift must have taken you hours to find. I appreciate it very much and I will always treasure both the gift and the warm feelings it represents.

                    Yours affectionately,

                    _____

                         1998 年9月24日

親愛的安娜：

   謝謝你送我這麼棒的禮物。妳一定花了不少時間，才找到這麼漂亮、迷人的禮物。我非常感謝，我一定會永遠珍藏這份禮物，以及它所代表的溫情。

                              上

USEFUL EXPRESSIONS ··············

* You couldn't possibly have selected a gift I like more.
  我非常喜歡你選的禮物。

* We love your present and want to thank you for the time and effort it must have cost you. 我們很喜歡你送的禮物，也謝謝你所花的心思與時間。

感謝祝賀結婚

May 15, 1998

Dear Martin,

Thank you for your letter about our recent wedding. Your congratulations were warmly received and very welcome. We would both like to thank you for the gift of support and good wishes.

Your friends,

1998 年 5 月 15 日

親愛的馬丁：

謝謝你寫給我們的新婚賀函。你的祝賀令我們倍感溫馨與歡喜。我們倆在此要感謝你的支持及祝福。

友

感謝祝賀生日

October 30, 1998

Dear John,

I appreciated the card you sent me. It was very kind of you to remember my birthday. I was very touched by your thoughtfulness and affection. I give you my best regards in return.

Your friend,

1998 年 10 月 30 日

親愛的約翰：

謝謝你寄給我的卡片，真感激你記得我的生日。對你的體貼及情誼，我深受感動，也同樣祝福你一切都好。

友

USEFUL EXPRESSIONS ⋯⋯⋯⋯⋯⋯

* Every year, my friends make me so happy on my birthday. 每年的生日朋友都讓我成為快樂的壽星。
* For your sincere wishes for my birthday, I thank you from the bottom of my heart.
  對於你誠心的祝壽，我衷心感激。

感謝祝賀畢業就業

July 6, 1998

Dear David,

　　Your letter concerning my recent graduation and subsequent position in my new company was most encouraging.　Your support is very important to me, and I will always remember your kindness wherever my new career takes me.

　　　　　　　　　　　　　　　　Yours sincerely,

　　　　　　　　　　　　　　　　1998 年 7 月 6 日

親愛的大衞：

　　你的來信恭賀我新近畢業，及隨獲新公司職位，令我無比的振奮。你的支持對我非常重要，不論我的職業生涯如何發展，我永遠都會記得你的好意。

　　　　　　　　　　　　　　　　　　　敬上

** subsequent 〔ˈsʌbsɪ͵kwɛnt〕 *adj*. 隨後的

感謝祝賀陞遷

June 25, 1998

Dear Roger,

It was very kind of you to write to me. Thank you for your best wishes; however, I am afraid to say that I do not deserve such congratulations, and I can only try my best to live up to your expectations.

Never fear, I will do my best.

Yours sincerely,

1998 年 6 月 25 日

親愛的羅傑：

非常感激你寫信給我。謝謝你的祝福，然而我恐怕自己擔當不起你的祝賀，我只能全力以赴，以不負你的厚望。

不用擔心，我會竭盡所有能力的。

敬上

** *live up to* 達到預期標準

與眾不同的男性英文名字......

Antony〔'æntənɪ〕安東尼	Kevin〔'kɛvɪn〕凱文
Arnold〔'ɑrnld〕阿諾	Larry〔'lærɪ〕賴瑞
Arthur〔'ɑrθə〕亞瑟	Lawrence〔'lɔrəns〕勞倫斯
Benjamin〔'bɛndʒəmən〕班傑明	Matthew〔'mæθju〕馬修
Brandon〔'brændən〕布蘭頓	Maurice〔'mɔrɪs〕墨利斯
Brian〔'braɪən〕布萊恩	Murphy〔'mɚfɪ〕墨菲
Carl〔kɑrl〕卡爾	Nelson〔'nɛlsn〕尼爾森
Charles〔tʃɑrlz〕查爾斯	Nicholas〔'nɪkləs〕尼古拉斯
Christopher〔'krɪstəfɚ〕克里斯多夫	Oliver〔'ɑləvɚ〕奧利佛
Daniel〔'dænjəl〕丹尼爾	Oscar〔'ɔskɚ〕奧斯卡
Dennis〔'dɛnɪs〕丹尼斯	Otto〔'ɑto〕歐特
Douglas〔'dʌgləs〕道格拉斯	Patrick〔'pætrɪk〕派屈克
Edward〔'ɛdwəd〕愛德華	Phil〔fɪl〕菲爾
Eugene〔jʊ'dʒin〕尤金	Quinton〔'kwɪntən〕昆頓
Frank〔fræŋk〕法蘭克	Roderick〔'rɑdərɪk〕羅德里克
Gary〔'gɛrɪ〕蓋瑞	Richard〔'rɪtʃəd〕理查
George〔dʒɔrdʒ〕喬治	Samuel〔'sæmjʊəl〕山米爾
Gregory〔'grɛgərɪ〕葛烈格里	Sidney〔'sɪdnɪ〕席德尼
Howard〔'hauəd〕霍爾德	Simon〔'saɪmən〕賽門
Hugh〔hju〕修	Terence〔'tɛrəns〕泰倫斯
Ian〔'iən〕伊安	Thomas〔'tɑməs〕湯瑪士
Isaac〔'aɪzək〕艾撒克	Timothy〔'tɪməθɪ〕提摩西
Jeremy〔'dʒɛrəmɪ〕傑瑞米	Ulysses〔jʊ'lɪsiz〕尤里西斯
Jesse〔'dʒɛsɪ〕賈西	Victor〔'vɪktə〕維克爾
Joseph〔'dʒozəf〕約瑟夫	Vincent〔'vɪnsnt〕文森
Keith〔kiθ〕凱斯	William〔'wɪljəm〕威廉
Kenneth〔'kɛnɪθ〕肯尼士	Wayne〔wen〕韋恩

高雅脫俗的女性英文名字 ||||||||||||||||||||

Agnes〔'ægnɪs〕艾格妮絲

Amelia〔ə'miljə〕艾蜜莉雅

Audrey〔'ɔdrɪ〕奧黛麗

Belinda〔bə'lɪndə〕碧琳達

Brook〔brʊk〕布魯克

Caroline〔'kærə,laɪn〕卡洛琳

Catherine〔'kæθərɪn〕凱薩琳

Christina〔krɪs'tinə〕克莉絲汀娜

Deborah〔'dɛbərə〕黛博拉

Denise〔də'niz〕丹妮絲

Edith〔'idɪθ〕伊蒂絲

Eunice〔'junɪs〕尤妮絲

Freda〔'fridə〕弗麗達

Frances〔'frænsɪs〕法蘭西絲

Gloria〔'glorɪə〕葛羅莉亞

Grace〔gres〕葛蕾絲

Hannah〔'hænə〕漢娜

Hilary〔'hɪlərɪ〕希拉蕊

Ida〔'aɪdə〕愛達

Ingrid〔'ɪŋgrɪd〕英格麗

Iris〔'aɪrɪs〕艾瑞絲

Jessica〔'dʒɛsɪkə〕潔西卡

Jocelyn〔'dʒɑslɪn〕賈思琳

Karen〔'kærən〕凱倫

Kay〔ke〕凱伊

Kelly〔'kɛlɪ〕凱莉

Lesley〔'lɛzlɪ〕雷思麗

Lydia〔'lɪdɪə〕莉蒂亞

Madeline〔'mædəlɪn〕麥德琳

Michelle〔mɪ'ʃɛl〕蜜雪兒

Monica〔'mɑnɪkə〕莫妮卡

Natalie〔'nætəlɪ〕娜姐莉

Nicole〔ni'kɔl〕妮可

Olivia〔o'lɪvɪə〕奧麗薇亞

Ophelia〔o'filjə〕奧菲麗亞

Page〔pedʒ〕佩姬

Phoebe〔'fibɪ〕菲比

Phoenix〔'finɪks〕菲妮克絲

Queena〔'kwinə〕昆娜

Rachel〔'retʃəl〕瑞秋

Roxanne〔rɑk'sæn〕羅珊

Sharon〔'ʃærən〕雪倫

Sheila〔'ʃilə〕席拉

Sylvia〔'sɪlvɪə〕西薇雅

Teresa〔tə'risə〕泰瑞莎

Tiffany〔'tɪfənɪ〕蒂芬妮

Ula〔'ulə〕鳥拉

Virginia〔və'dʒɪnjə〕維琴妮亞

Vivien〔'vɪvɪən〕薇安

Wanda〔'wɑndə〕汪妲

Wendy〔'wɛndɪ〕溫蒂

Yolanda〔jo'lændə〕尤蓮達

Yvonne〔ɪ'vɑn〕伊芳

Zora〔'zorə〕索拉

 請求赴約

January 14, 1998

Dear Anna,

    Since we met, I have been thinking about you more and more. I can't get the image of your face out of my mind. After such a fun evening dancing, I was so excited that I tossed and turned all night.

    This Saturday we are all going out to see a movie. I would be so happy if you could go with me. Please do say you will come and let me know as soon as possible.

Yours truly,

Dating

1998 年 1 月 14 日

親愛的安娜：

　　自從我們認識後，我對你的思念愈益加深。我無法將你的臉龐，自我腦海中揮去。在共舞度過歡愉的夜晚後，我是如此的興奮，整夜輾轉難眠。

　　這星期六我們打算去看電影，如果妳能與我同行，我將感到快樂。請告訴我妳會來，並儘快讓我知道妳的回覆。

上

INFORMATION ··············

　　中文的「喜歡」可英譯成 *love* 或 *like* 。 like 是指對人或物有親切感，而 love 則表示強烈的情感與愛意。所以，第一次向對方示愛時，最好選用 *I like you.* 才不會嚇走對方。
　　love 也有另一層的涵意，若有人向你借筆記本，歸還時他可能送上一句 *Oh, I love you!* 這時可別陶醉，他指的是 *Thank you.*

給女友

March 7, 1998

My dearest Mary,

I think of you constantly and can't wait
to return home. I have so many things I
wish to say to you but which I could never
put down on paper. I love you and miss you
every minute we are apart.

Every time I receive one of your letters,
I tear it open in my eagerness to hear from
you. When I read your letters, it is as if I
am with you. To hear your voice again is what
I look forward to.

I promise I will be back soon. Until
then, please write often.

Your devoted boyfriend,

To a Girlfriend

1998 年 3 月 7 日

我最親愛的瑪麗：

　　我一直想著妳，也等不及想要回家。我有好多話想對妳說，但却無從用文字表達起。在我們分離的每一刻，我一直愛著妳，念著妳。

　　每次我收到妳的來信，都迫不及待地拆閱，好得知妳的消息。當我讀妳的信時，就彷彿與妳同在。而今我所期待的，就是能再聽見妳的聲音。

　　我保證我很快就會回來。在我回來之前，請多寫信給我。

　　　　　　　　　　　　　　　　你最忠實的男友

** constantly〔'kɑnstəntlɪ〕*adv.* 不斷地

♡ 雋永情詩

Love is love for evermore.　　愛是天長地久。
　　　　— Tennyson　　　　　　　　一丹尼生

給男友

February 8, 1998

Darling John,

Your letter brought so much joy to me, so I'll reply as quickly as possible. Every moment with you is so memorable and joyful that a letter just can't compare. Now, while we are apart, this letter will have to do.

Every night before I go to bed, I look at your photo and the teddy bear you won for me at the amusement park. Do you still remember that afternoon? It is still the best of all our good memories for me.

Do hurry back, I miss you and I can't wait to see you again. Until then please write to me.

With all my love,

To a Boyfriend

1998 年 2 月 8 日

約翰吾愛：

　　你的來信帶給我無比的喜悅，所以我要儘快的回信。與你共度的每一刻，都是如此令人難忘及愉快，一封信根本無法比擬。然而如今我們分隔二地，只好以此信來訴衷曲。

　　我每晚入睡前，都會看著你的相片，及你在遊樂場爲我贏來的玩具熊。你還記得那天下午嗎？在我們所有美好回憶中，那天對我來說還是最溫馨的。

　　儘快歸來。我好想你，迫不及待地要與你相見。在你回來前這段期間，請寫信給我。

獻上我所有的愛

** amusement park　遊樂場

求婚信

February 14, 1998

Dear Susanna,

Over the past few weeks I have been working myself up to ask you an important question. Over the years we have become closer and closer and now you mean so much to me. The more we are together, the more certain I am of my feelings.

No doubt by now you can guess what I am driving at, Susanna, will you marry me? I love you more than I can say and I believe that together we would be happier than words could describe. I am suffering deeply from the agony of not knowing what your answer will be. Please let me know as soon as possible.

I remain your devoted friend,

Marriage Proposal

1998 年 2 月 14 日

親愛的蘇珊娜：

　　這幾週來，我一直替自己打氣要問妳一個重要的問題。這些年來，我們已越來越親密。而今，妳對我來說，是如此地重要。我們每多一點相處，我就更確定自己的感情。

　　相信妳現在必定能猜到我打算說什麼了。蘇珊娜，妳願意嫁給我嗎？我對妳的愛，勝過言語所能形容，我相信，妳我若能長相廝守，其幸福亦絕非筆墨所能形容。我現在深深苦於妳會給我什麼樣的答覆。請儘快給我回音。

　　　　　　　　　　　　　　永遠是妳最忠實的朋友

** work up 激動　　　***drive at*** 用意所在
agony〔ˊæɡənɪ〕*n.* 痛苦

 接受求婚

February 17, 1998

Dear Martin,

When I read your letter last night, it made me happier than I had ever been. Yes, of course I will marry you, the sooner the better.

I can't tell you how I have dreamt of this moment and now you have made me the happiest girl on earth. Come around straightaway tomorrow and we'll start to make plans.

Your future wife,

Accepting a Marriage Proposal

1998 年 2 月 17 日

親愛的馬丁：

　　昨晚讀你的信時，我感到前所未有的快樂。是
的，我當然願意嫁給你，愈快愈好。

　　我無法向你描述，我是如何夢想著這一刻，而
現在，你已使我成為全世界最幸福的女孩。明天就
直接來我這兒，我們開始來好好計劃。

你的準老婆

♡ 雋永情詩

I give you my hand !	我給了你我的手
I give you my love more	給了你比金錢
precious than money.	還寶貴的愛
Will you give me yourself?	你願意將你交給我嗎?
Will you come travel with me	你願意和我繼續人生之旅嗎?
Shall we stick by each other	我們可以今生今世
as long as we live?	長相廝守嗎?

—Walt Whitman　　　　　　　　　　　　　　—惠特曼

婉拒求婚

February 17, 1998

Dear Martin,

I was distressed when I read your proposal last night. Not because the idea of marrying you upset me but because of the knowledge of the sadness my refusal will cause you. I am flattered that you asked me to be your wife, but I am afraid that is not possible. I hope that despite all this we will remain good friends.

Your sincerely,

1998年2月17日

親愛的馬丁：

我昨晚讀你的求婚信時，感到很苦惱。並不是嫁給你這個主意帶給我困擾，而是我知道我的拒絕，將會令你難過。你的求婚讓我受寵若驚，然而我恐怕那是不太可能的。我希望，不管怎麼樣，我們依舊是好朋友。

敬上

EVERLASTING SAYINGS ABOUT LOVE

不朽的情話

O, my love is like a red, red rose
   That's newly sprung in June.
O, my love is like the melodie
   That's sweetly play'd in tune.
                    — *Burns*

喔，我的愛人像一朵紅紅的玫瑰，
   新開於六月；
喔，我的愛人如一首美妙的樂曲，
   奏出悅耳的旋律。
                    —伯恩斯

Thou wast all that to me, love,
   For which my soul pine:
A green isle in the sea, love,
   A fountain and a shrine.
                — *Edgar Allan Poe*

你是我的所有，愛人，
   我的靈魂為你憔悴：
你是海中翠綠的島嶼，愛人，
   你是泉源，是聖殿。
                    —愛倫坡

Doubt thou the stars are fire;
   Doubt that the sun doth move;
Doubt truth to be a liar;
   But never doubt I love.
                — *Shakespeare*

你可以懷疑星星是火光；
   懷疑太陽移動了；
懷疑真理是謊言；
   但是，請不要懷疑我的愛。
                    —莎士比亞

If love were what the rose is,
And I were like the leaf,
Our lives would grow together
In sad or singing weather.
                — *Swinburne*

如果情人是玫瑰，
我便是那片葉，
我們的生命將一起成長
無論天氣陰晴。
                    —史因伯恩

So let our love as endless prove,
And pure as gold for ever.
                — *Robert Herrick*

讓我們的愛成為永恆，
永遠純如黃金。
                    —羅伯‧海瑞克

We are all born for love; it is the
principle of existence and its
only end.
   — *Benjamin Disraeli*

我們生來為愛；它是生存的原則和
唯一的目的。
    —班哲明‧迪士瑞里

To love is to believe, to hope, to
know; 'Tis an essay, a taste of
Heaven Below!
   — *Edmund Waller*

愛是相信、希望、了解；它是一篇
文章，它使你領略極樂世界的歡
欣。
    —愛德蒙‧瓦勒

Shall I compare thee to a summer's day?
Thou art more lovely and more temperate.
   — *Shakespeare*

我可以將你比做夏日嗎？
你比夏日更可愛，你比夏日更溫和。
    —莎士比亞

One can't choose when one is going
to love.
   — *Henrik Ibsen*

要愛的時候難以抉擇。
    —亨利‧易卜生

Where love is, there's no lack.
   — *Richard Brome*

有愛的地方就沒有匱乏。
    —理查‧布羅米

It's love, it's love that makes the world
go round.
   — *Unknown*

是愛，是愛使世界運轉不息。
    —佚名

O tell her, brief is life but love is long.
   — *Tennyson*

喔，告訴她，生命短暫但是愛情長久。
    —丹尼生

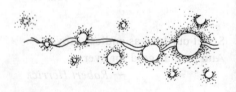

工作類信函

CHAPTER

3

　　教育的普及，加上大眾學習意願的高漲，形成了社會上人才供過於求的現象。究竟如何才能在眾多人才中脫穎而出呢？一份簡潔、明確的履歷表，無疑是邁向成功的第一步。在本章的開頭，我們就為讀者介紹如何寫一份漂亮的英文履歷表。在接下的單元裡，我們將介紹相關的求職信函，與履歷表一氣呵成，是求職致勝的黃金組合。最後，我們列舉工作中應對進退的信函，如要求加薪、辭呈等。人生有許多戰役要打，我們希望本章的製作能助您在事業聖戰中旗開得勝。

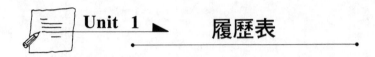

Unit 1 ▶ 履歷表

履歷表是應徵工作時，不可或缺的重要文件，它可達到自我推銷的目的，進而爭取面試的機會。英文履歷表沒有特定的格式，可隨個人的喜好來寫，但仍需掌握下列重點：

- ◉ 積極表現自己的才能
- ◉ 具體寫出業績與成果
- ◉ 注意格式的整體性
- ◉ 重要的資料先寫出來
- ◉ 挑選特殊的資料來寫

一份完整的履歷表應包含：(1)個人資料，(2)希望的職務，(3)工作經驗，(4)學歷，(5)課外活動，(6)資格技能幾項。

(1) **個人資料**（ Personal Information ）：籍貫、婚姻狀況、性別、生日、地址、電話等都可列出，但應酌量，不需詳細陳述。

(2) **希望的職務**（ Job Objective ）：在履歷表開頭的位置，具體而扼要的寫出所希望的職務，可讓雇主明瞭你的目標，如：Personnel recruitment（人事招募）就比 Personnel work（人事工作）來得具體。對社會新鮮人而言，可選擇較彈性的說法，才不會予人好高騖遠的印象，如：Entry-level position in a sales department（業務部門的初級職位）。

(3) **工作經驗**（ Work Experience ）：多數的公司喜歡錄取有經驗的應徵者，所以曾任職的公司**名稱、服務期間、職務**都需寫清楚。一般而言，目前的工作是最重要的，所以寫在前頭，且要寫得最詳細。若以前的經歷和應徵的工作有密切關連，則先寫該職務。

(4) **學歷**（Education）：剛踏出校園的社會新鮮人，由於社會經驗少，學歷就顯得重要。因此，最好將學歷擺在前面。若在校成績優異，曾經得獎，也可列出來。學歷的書寫順序是由近往回推。

(5) **課外活動**（Extracurricular Activities）：有些公司非常重視課外活動，因為從中可看出人際關係與領導能力。興趣可反映性格，若個人興趣與應徵工作有關，都可列出來，讓雇主加深印象。

(6) **資格技能**（Technical Qualifications／Special Skills）：擁有特殊技能可增加錄取的機會，因此不必謙虛隱藏實力。有關高普考、特考等資格檢定證明，語言、電腦方面的專才，甚至著作、專利權都可以寫。

　　履歷表不宜繁瑣冗長，理想的長度是一至二頁，若沒有指定手寫，則用打字。紙張的規格是**八開（A4）的白紙**，左右至少留白2公分，上下至少空2.5公分，每寫完一項都要空行。標題的部份可用大寫字體，或是畫底線的方式，使之醒目。

Résumé

‖‖

John Lin

18, Lane 12, Hsinsheng S. Rd. , Sec. 2

Taipei, Taiwan, R.O.C.

Telephone : (02) 721-3621

OBJECTIVE : Position as Design Engineer in Engineering
Department

WORK EXPERIENCE

8/90-7/94	Senior Engineer at Lin and Chang Hydraulic Engineering Company producing designs for dams and other hydraulic systems.
7/85-8/90	Engineer with the South Chia-nan Irrigation Association Working with the design and maintanence of irrigation system.
7/81-7/85	Sales Clerk, Wellcome Supermarket Hsintien. Employed part time supporting my studies.

EDUCATION

1985	B. S. Civil Engineering National Taiwan University.
1978-1981	Kaohsiung High School

履 歷 表

||||||||||||||||||||||||||||||||||||||||||||||||||||||||||||||||||||||||||||||||||||||||||||||||||||||||||||||||||||||

林約翰

中華民國台灣省台北市新生南路二段12巷18號

電話：（02）721-3621

希望職位：工程部門之設計工程師

工作經歷

8/90-7/94　　林張水力工程公司之資深工程師，負責水壩及
　　　　　　其他水力系統的設計。

7/85-8/90　　嘉南灌溉工會工程師。負責灌溉系統的設計及
　　　　　　維修。

7/81-7/85　　頂好超級市場新店店售貨員。兼職型態以負擔
　　　　　　學費。

教　育

1985　　　　國立台灣大學土木工程學士

1978-1981　　就讀高雄中學

EXTRACURRICULAR ACTIVITIES

9/82-12/85   Volunteer deputy chairman of the Taiwan Engineering Students Association, Taipei branch, a non-profit organization dedicated to fostering the study of Civil Engineering and foreign links with industry and government.

1981-1985   Member of Computer Research Club, National Taiwan University.

1979-1981   President of Mathematics Club, Kaohsiung High School.

HOBBIES

Computer games, Baseball, Swimming

PERSONAL DATA

Born : May 12, 1963 in Taichung
Health : Excellent
Marital Status : Single

課外活動

9/82-12/85　台灣工程系學生協會台北分會志願副主席。爲一非營利組織，致力於提升土木工程研究，以及與工業界、政府的交流。

1981-1985　台灣大學計算機研究社社員

1979-1981　高雄中學數學社社長

興　趣

電腦遊戲、棒球、游泳

個人資料

出生：1963年5月12日，台中
健康：良好
婚姻狀況：未婚

** hydraulic〔haɪˋdrɔlɪk〕*adj.* 水力的
irrigation〔͵ɪrəˋgeʃən〕*n.* 灌溉
maintanence〔ˋmentənəns〕*n.* 維持
extracurricular〔͵ɛkstrəkəˋrɪkjələ〕*adj.* 課外的
deputy〔ˋdɛpjətɪ〕*adj.* 副的　　foster〔ˋfɔstə〕*v.* 鼓勵
marital〔ˋmærətḷ〕*adj.* 婚姻的

Résumé

‖‖

Name : Susanna H. Y. Tang

Address : 7th Floor, 36, Lane 126, Nanking East Road,
Section 5, Taipei, Taiwan, R.O.C.

Date of Birth : July 12, 1936

Nationality : Taiwan, R.O.C.

Marital Status : Married.

Sex : Female

POSITION APPLIED FOR

Senior Economic Advisor, Citibank

PROFESSIONAL EXPERIENCE

From 1966 to 1975 I was an Economic Advisor to the Ministry of Finance, R.O.C. In this role I sat on committees dealing with the economic policy and future economic development of the R.O.C.

From 1975 to 1994 I was Vice-President of Economic Forecasting at a Washington-based think tank, in the United States. During this period we advised policy makers on the likely implications of macro-economic reforms and international finance developments.

履 歷 表

IIIIIIIIIIIIIIIIIIIIIIIIIIIIIIIIIIIIIIIIIIIIIIIIIIIIIIIIIIIIIIIIIIIIIIIIIIII

姓　　名：蘇珊娜H. Y. 唐

地　　址：中華民國台灣省台北市南京東路五段126巷36號7樓

出生日期：1936年7月12日

國　　籍：中華民國台灣

婚　　姻：已婚。

性　　別：女

應徵職位
　　花旗銀行資深經濟顧問

工作經歷
　　自1966年至1975年，我任職於中華民國財政部，為經濟顧問。在此職位，我於委員會內處理台灣的經濟政策，及未來經濟發展事宜。

　　自1975至1994年，我任職美國經濟預測華盛頓智囊團的副主席。在此期間，我們提供決策者有關總體經濟改革、以及國際金融發展的可能走向。

EDUCATIONAL BACKGROUND

1968	Ph. D. Macro-economic Reform University of Chicago, Ill.
1963	M. S., Economics, Yale, Conn.
1961	B. S. National Taiwan University
1957	Graduated from First Girls' High School, Taipei, Taiwan, R.O.C.

PUBLICATIONS

" Where Next for Unions? " published 1969 — Journal of Economic Mathematics — New York

" Reform and the Oil Shock " published 1977 — Applied Economics — Chicago

" Macro-economic Reform into the Next Century " 651 pgs, published 1981 by Yale University Press, Conn.

學　歷

| 1968 | 伊利諾州芝加哥大學總體經濟改革博士 |

1963	康乃狄克州耶魯大學經濟碩士
1961	國立台灣大學學士
1957	台灣台北第一女子高級中學畢業

著　作

聯盟下步何處去？（1969），紐約：「經濟數學月刊」

改革與石油恐慌（1977），芝加哥：「應用經濟學」

邁向下一世紀總體經濟改革651頁（1981），耶魯大學發行

** ministry〔'mɪnɪstrɪ〕*n.* 部　　　*sit on* 擔任
committee〔kə'mɪtɪ〕*n.* 委員會　*think tank* 智囊團
implication〔ɪmplɪ'keʃən〕*n.* 含意
Ph. D. 是 Doctor of Philosophy（博士）的縮寫
journal〔'dʒɝnḷ〕*n.* 刊物

全國大學暨學院校名英譯表

英　　文　　校　　名	中　文　校　名
National Taiwan University	國立台灣大學
National Tsing Hua University	國立清華大學
National Chiao Tung University	國立交通大學
National Chengchi University	國立政治大學
National Cheng Kung University	國立成功大學
National Chunghsing University	國立中興大學
National Sun Yat-Sen University	國立中山大學
National Central University	國立中央大學
National Chung Cheng University	國立中正大學
National Yang Ming University	國立陽明大學
National Taiwan Ocean University	國立台灣海洋大學
National Taiwan Normal University	國立台灣師範大學
National Changhua Normal University	國立彰化師範大學
National Kaohsiung Normal University	國立高雄師範大學
National Open University	國立空中大學
Tunghai University	東海大學
Fu Jen Catholic University	輔仁大學
Soochow University	東吳大學
Tamkang University	淡江大學
Feng Chia University	逢甲大學
Chung Yuan Christian University	中原大學
Chinese Culture University	中國文化大學

英　文　校　名	中　文　校　名
Providence University	靜宜大學
Taipei Medical College	台北醫學院
China Medical College	中國醫藥學院
Kaohsiung Medical College	高雄醫學院
Chung Shan Medical & Dental College	中山醫學院
Tzu Chi College of Medicine	慈濟醫學院
Chang Gung College of Medicine and Technology	長庚醫學暨工程學院
National Defense Medical College	國防醫學院
National Taipei College of Nursing	國立台北護理學院
National Taipei Teachers College	國立台北師範學院
National Hsinchu Teachers College	國立新竹師範學院
National Hualien Teachers College	國立花蓮師範學院
National Taichung Teachers College	國立台中師範學院
National Chiayi Teachers College	國立嘉義師範學院
National Tainan Teachers College	國立台南師範學院
National Pingtung Teachers College	國立屏東師範學院
National Taitung Teachers College	國立台東師範學院
Taipei Municipal Teachers College	台北市立師範學院
Tatung Institute of Technology	大同工學院
Chung-Hua Institute of Technology	中華工學院
Da-Yeh Institute of Technology	大葉工學院
Yuan-Ze Institute of Technology	元智工學院
Kaohsiung Polytechnic Institue	高雄工學院
National Taiwan Institute of Technology	國立台灣工業技術學院

英　文　校　名	中　文　校　名
National Yunlin Institute of Technology	國立雲林技術學院
National Pingtung Polytechnic Institute	國立屏東技術學院
National Institute of the Arts	國立藝術學院
Hua Fan College of Humanities and Technology	華梵人文科技學院
The World College of Journalism and Communications	世界新聞傳播學院
Shih Chien College	實踐管理設計學院
Tamsui Oxford College	淡水工商管理學院
Ming Chuan College	銘傳管理學院
National College of Physical Education and Sports	國立體育學院
Central Police College	中央警官學校
Christ's College	基督書院

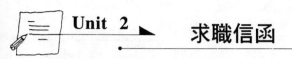

Unit 2 ▶ 求職信函

自傳（*Autobiography*）

　　理想的自傳應提及個人資料、學歷、工作經驗、理想與抱負等。履歷表與自傳常有重疊，前者是條列式的說明，而後者可說是敍述性的補充。因此，撰寫自傳時，可**挑選重點**，讓雇主加深印象。對剛踏出校園的畢業生來說，履歷表起不了大作用，因此，不妨在自傳上多花點工夫。

應徵函（*Application Letter*）

　　雇主很可能在不同的報紙上刊登求才廣告，所以應徵函需提及所見到的廣告。同理，一則廣告內可能徵求各類的人才，因此，也該把應徵的工作項目寫出來。信中需說明**應徵的理由**，以及簡略的**學經歷**（可附寄履歷表、自傳）。若資歷稍嫌不足，可多著墨個人的熱忱與個性，以及學習的意願。

推薦函（*Recommendation Letter*）

　　師長或前雇主最常被要求寫推薦函。如果要求者並無嚴重過錯，為人也誠懇勤奮，基於舊日情誼，都該幫忙，為他們寫些正面的評價。但也不能熱心過度，寫些不符實情的內容，否則不僅有違誠信原則，還可能為受薦者帶來困擾。有些雇主會寫信給推薦人，詢問有關應徵者的資料。基於禮貌，有必要回覆，若置之不理，極可能影響受薦者的錄取。

自傳

Autobiography

I was born and raised in Chiayi, a city in the central part of Western Taiwan, the third son of a family of four children. My father is now manager of a leading local bank and my mother teaches at a high school.

My family all belong to the Methodist faith and I have been raised to be a devoted Christian. Since I was in high school, I have been involved in numerous church organizations and activities, culminating in my election as President of our local youth group.

During my high school years I studied very hard, earned excellent grades and performed well enough in the Joint College Entrance Examinations to attend the prestigious National Taiwan University. I am now in my final year in the Business Administration Department and I expect to graduate in the next few months.

I would further like to point out that I am a responsible, hard working and serious person who would have a great effect on your company's performance. Thank you for your serious consideration of my application.

Autobiography

　　我生長於台灣中西部的嘉義市，在家中四個子女中排行老三。家父現任本地一主要銀行經理，家母是中學老師。

　　我們全家都屬於衛理教派，我自己是一名虔誠的基督徒。我在中學時，參與了許多教會團契與活動，最後並當選我們當地青年團契的主席。

　　我高中時非常用功，因此成績優異，並在大學聯考中考取了校譽卓著的台灣大學。我現在就讀於工管系四年級，再幾個月就畢業了。

　　此外我想聲明的是，我負責、勤勉、認真，相信必能使貴公司的業務蒸蒸日上。感謝您對我的應徵詳加考慮。

＊＊ Methodist〔ˈmɛθədɪst〕*n.* 衛理教徒
　　（亦有人稱美以美教徒）
　　culminate〔ˈkʌlməˌnet〕*v.* 達到顛峰，
　　常與 in 連用
　　prestigious〔prɛsˈtɪdʒɪəs〕*adj.* 有聲望的

自薦函

July 15, 1998

Dear Sir,

It has recently been brought to my attention that you are looking for an experienced Quality Control Supervisor. I have over twelve years of experience in this field and with systems very similar to yours.

I am enclosing some relevant documents concerning my experience in this work. I would appreciate an opportunity to see you and your factory. If you feel an interview is appropriate, please contact me to arrange a suitable time.

Yours sincerely,

Self-Recommendation

1998 年 7 月 15 日

敬啓者：

　　我最近注意到您在徵求有經驗的品管督導，而我對這一行、對和貴廠極類似的系統，已有十二年以上的經驗。

　　隨函附上有關我在這行經歷的相關資料。衷心盼望能有機會與您會面，並參觀貴工廠。如果您認爲宜於有個面談的話，請與我聯絡以安排適當的時間。

敬上

** supervisor〔͵sjupəˊvaɪzə〕*n.* 管理者
document〔ˊdɑkjə͵mənt〕*n.* 文件

SUGGESTIONS ·············

　　自薦函是主動出擊，因此要突顯自己的長才，但也不宜自恃過高，語氣要謙虛客氣。隨函可附上有關資料，如履歷表、自傳等。

應徵函

July 4, 1998

Dear Sir,

  I saw your advertisement in the China Post today looking for an Administrative Assistant with some experience in working at a construction and engineering company, and I would like to apply for the position. I am 28 years old, single, and have six years experience in my present position. I am able to provide references for the last eleven years and I have a thorough knowledge of office routine.

  I would expect a salary of $400,000 a year. I'm looking forward to hearing from you.

Yours sincerely,

Job Application

1998 年 7 月 4 日

敬啓者：

　　我看到貴公司在今天中國郵報上的廣告，要找一名
有建設工程公司工作經驗的行政助理，我想要應徵該職
位。我現年二十八歲，未婚，在現職已有六年的經驗。
我過去十一年來都是有稽可考，也非常熟悉辦公程序。

　　我希望的待遇是年薪四十萬元。期盼聽到您的回音。

敬上

** advertisement〔ædvəˈtaɪzmənt〕 *n.* 廣告（簡寫爲ad）
　　routine〔ruˈtin〕 *n.* 例行工作
　　reference〔ˈrɛfərəns〕 *n.* 證明書

SUGGESTIONS ················

　　有些公司會請應徵者開出希望待遇，因此可先打聽一番，參
照一般行情，以免獅子大開口，喪失錄取的機會。

 **通知面試**

July 11, 1998

Dear Mr. Wang

In reply to your application for the position advertised in *The China Post* for an Administrative Assistant (Clerk Level Two), I would like to ask you to attend a final interview here at 10: 30 a. m. tomorrow. Should your references and abilities be satisfactory, I have no doubt that we will be happy to offer you the position.

Yours sincerely,

1998 年 7 月 11 日

王先生：

關於中國郵報上所徵求的行政助理一職(二級職員)，你的應徵申請我們已收到。我想請你於明早十點半來此參加最後的面試。如果你的資歷及能力令人滿意，無疑的我們會很樂意聘請你。

敬上

通知未獲錄取

July 11, 1998

Dear Mr. Wang

In reply to your application of July 4th, I regret to inform you that the position has already been filled. However we will be filing your application, should a further vacancy occur.

Yours sincerely,

1998 年 7 月 11 日

王先生：

關於您七月四日的應徵信，我很遺憾須通知您，該職位已被遞補了。不過我們會將您的資料建檔，將來若有空缺會再通知您。

敬上

** vacancy〔ˈvekənsɪ〕n. 空缺

請求推薦

June 23, 1998

Dear Sir,

I am now in the process of applying for a position in a well-established law firm and would therefore like to ask you to provide me with a letter of recommendation. I was employed by your company for seven years during which time my work brought nothing but praise. If you could provide me with such a letter, I would be very grateful.

Yours sincerely,

1998 年 6 月 23 日

敬愛的先生：

我目前正應徵一家頗具規模法律公司的職位，因此想有勞您幫我寫封推薦函。我在貴公司服務了七年，期間我的表現一直受到賞識。若能蒙您的推薦，我會相當感激。

敬上

推薦函

June 30, 1998

Dear Sir,

Mr. Smith was employed with this company for a period of seven years during which time he worked directly under me.　I found Mr. Smith a thoroughly capable worker whose performance was never less than satisfactory.　He is by nature honest and brings to his work dedication, enthusiasm and energy.　His resignation was a great loss to this company.

Sincerely yours,

1998 年 6 月 30 日

敬啓者：

　　史密斯先生在敝公司任職了七年，直屬於我的部門。史先生是個十足的人才，他的表現一向令人滿意。他生性誠實、工作賣力，他的離職是敝公司的一大損失。

敬上

** **by nature** 生性　　dedication〔͵dɛdə'keʃən〕 *n*. 奉獻
enthusiasm〔ɪn'θjuzɪ͵æzəm〕 *n*. 熱忱
resignation〔͵rɛzɪg'neʃən〕 *n*. 辭職

聘書

July 1, 1998

Dear Mr. Smith,

Thank you for your prompt attendance for your interview last Thursday.

It is with great pleasure that we confirm our offer of the position of Sales Director in our company.

Enclosed you will find two copies of your contract. Please sign and return one copy as soon as possible.

Your presence at work on Monday is both expected and a source of pleasure to the Board.

Yours Sincerely,

Employment

1998 年 7 月 1 日

親愛的史密斯先生：

感謝您上週四隨即來參加面試。

我很高興能向您證實，您已獲得本公司業務主任的職位。

隨函附上兩份合約書的影本。請簽名後將其中一份儘速寄回。

董事會欣然期待您週一能到職上任。

敬上

** board〔bɔrd〕*n.* 董事會

⚓ 公司裏的職稱

President; Chairman of the Board 董事長
Director 董事　　　　　　General manager 總經理
Manager 經理　　　　　　Manageress 女經理
Assistant Manager 副理　　Sales Manager 業務經理
Section Manager 課長　　　Advisor 顧問

 **請求加薪**

June 20, 1998

Dear Sir,

I have now been working at this company for fifteen months and during that time I believe my performance has been more than adequate.

When I first took this position, it was my understanding that my salary would gradually increase to $400,000. My salary now stands at $360,000. Therefore, I would like to ask for a raise in my salary, and I hope that this proposal will be looked on favorably.

Yours sincerely,

Asking for a Raise

1998 年 6 月 20 日

親愛的先生：

　　至今我已在公司服務達十五個月，在這段期間，我相信我的表現應是可圈可點。

　　我當初接下這職位時，就我所知，我的薪水會逐漸調到年薪四十萬元，而我目前的薪水是三十六萬元，所以我想要求加薪。我希望這項提議能獲支持。

敬上

SUGGESTIONS ··················

　　在工作崗位久了，都會有加薪或升職的打算，除非已準備離職，否則不宜採取威脅的手段。要求時得根據事實，表示自己的工作量增加，或按照合約，應該得到額外報酬或升等，切忌以資歷為藉口，以免令上司反感。

同意加薪

June 25, 1998

Dear Mr. Chen,

I received your letter asking for a raise and am pleased to inform you that your request has been granted. Your salary will be immediately raised from $360,000 to 400,000 a year. Furthermore as your work has been satisfactory, you can look forward to further salary increases at regular intervals.

Yours truly,

1998 年 6 月 25 日

陳先生：

我收到你要求加薪的信，也很高興通知你，你的要求獲得批准。你的年薪即日起由三十六萬元調至四十萬元。此外，由於你的工作一直很令人滿意，你在未來固定的期間，都可獲得加薪。

上

** interval〔'ɪntəvl〕 *n.* 期間

 **拒絕加薪**

June 25, 1998

Dear Mr. Chen.

I regret to inform you that, given the decline in company profit over the past year, I am unable to grant you an increase in salary at this time. As far as your work is concerned, it is satisfactory and, if business improves in the next six months, I'll be happy to increase your salary to at least 400,000, as per our original agreement.

Yours truly,

1998 年 6 月 25 日

陳先生：

很遺憾得通知你，鑑於公司一年來營運不佳，我無法在此時准許你加薪。你的工作本身令人滿意，如果公司半年內業績好轉，我會很樂意按照我們原先的協定，至少將你的薪水調高到四十萬元。

上

** as per 是口語用法，相當於 **according to** 。

辭呈

September 18, 1998

Dear Sir,

I am sorry to inform you that I am giving formal notice of the termination of my services, as of one month from today. Unfortunately I can no longer continue in my present position or with this company and I am leaving to take up a position in Boston.

Despite giving such notice, I would like to thank you for your past kindness toward me and express my sorrow that the circumstances do not permit me to remain with your company.

Yours sincerely,

Job Resignation

1998 年 9 月 18 日

敬愛的先生：

　　我很遺憾要通知您，我正式提出辭呈，從今天起一個月後生效。我很抱歉無法在現職或公司待下去，因爲我要前往波士頓一家公司任職。

　　雖然提出這樣的通知，我仍要感謝您過去對我親切的照顧，也要在此表達，我很遺憾環境不允許我繼續留在貴公司。

　　　　　　　　　　　　　　　　　敬上

** take up 有許多意思，在這裏是作「從事」解，其他常見的用法有：This work takes up too much time.（這工作佔去太多時間）。I'll take up my story.（我繼續講故事）。

准許辭職

September 20, 1998

Dear Mr. Wang,

It was with much sorrow that I read your letter announcing your desire to leave this company. I will naturally accept it, as of October 18.

I would like to offer my best wishes for your future career. I would be happy to provide any references or letters of recommendation that you may require.

Yours truly,

Job Resignation

1998 年 9 月 20 日

親愛的王先生：

　　讀了你的辭呈後，讓我非常遺憾。我當然會接受，從 10 月 18 日起生效。

　　我祝你前途光明燦爛，我也樂意提供你所需要的擔保或是推薦信。

上

函公司裏的單位

Main Office; Head Office; Headquarters 總公司
Branch Office 分公司　　　　　Plant; Factory 工廠
Public Relations Department 公關部
General Affairs Department 總務部
Business Department 營業部　　Publicity Department 宣傳部門
Finance Department 財務部　　Files Department 文書部
Accounting Section 會計課　　Administrative Section 管理課
Personnel Office 人事室　　　Planning Office 企畫室

 警告職員

October 4, 1998

Dear Mr. Chang,

I am sorry to inform you that your recent behavior has fallen short of what is expected from our employees.

Both the quantity and quality of your
work have declined, and you do not show the
degree of enthusiasm and motivation you did
when you were first employed here. Furthermore you have tended to arrive late and leave
early.

This present behavior is far from satisfactory and unless there is an improvement,
I shall have no other alternative but to ter-
minate your employment.

Yours truly,

Remonstration

1998 年 10 月 4 日

親愛的張先生：

　我很遺憾要通知你，你近來的表現，已低於我們所期待的員工水準。

　你工作的質與量都退步了，也缺乏初進公司時的熱忱與動力，此外，也經常遲到早退。

　你目前的表現，相當令人不滿意，除非能有所改進，否則我別無選擇，只能請你另謀高就了。

敬上

** behavior〔bɪˋhevjɚ〕*n*. 行為　　***fall short*** 短缺
　decline〔dɪˋklaɪn〕*v*. 減低
　motivation〔͵motəˋveʃən〕*n*. 動力
　alternative〔ɔlˋtɝnətɪv〕*n*. 選擇

 職員辯白

October 6, 1998

Dear Mr. Smith,

After reading your letter of September 2nd, I am afraid I have to admit the accuracy of your objections.

I am aware that my work has not been up to standard recently and the only excuse I can offer is that I have not been feeling well lately.

I can assure you that such behavior will not continue and I shall try to make up for my recent shortcomings.

Yours sincerely,

NOTES

1. objection 〔əb'dʒɛkʃən〕 *n.* 異議
2. shortcoming 〔'ʃɔrt'kʌmɪŋ〕 *n.*
   缺點

SUGGESTIONS

工作時日久了，都難免會罹患職業倦怠症，上班時可能提不起勁來，工作表現也未如人意。面對上司的指責，可以身體不適暫作爲藉口。若想保住飯碗，得好好加把勁，試著從舊有的工作裏，找出新意來。

Apologies

1998 年 10 月 6 日

親愛的史密斯先生：

讀了您九月二日的信函，我恐怕得承認您的指責完全正確。

我知道我最近的工作表現未達標準，我唯一能提出的理由是我最近人不大舒服。

我可以向您保證，這種行爲不會再持續下去，我會儘力彌補近來的過失。

敬上

辭退職員

October 15, 1998

Dear Mr. Roberts,

Following several warnings about the declining standard of your work, there has been no improvement at all. It is therefore apparent that your continued presence with us is no longer desirable. This is formal notice of the termination of your employment at this company effective three months from today as required under the Employment and Services Act.

Yours sincerely,

1998 年 10 月 15 日

羅伯茲先生：

經過多次的警告，你工作表現下滑的情形絲毫沒有改善，因此，我們已無意繼續留你在公司。這是解聘你的正式通知，依照就職服務法案，自即日起三個月後生效。

敬上

學校類信函

當您計畫出國留學時,除了思考選校、選系的問題外,必定也會爲該如何撰寫申請函、推薦函、讀書計畫……等留學文件而苦惱不已。雖然坊間有不少留學機構代人申請學校、撰寫諸類文件,然而所費不貲,並非人人都有這筆預算。其實這類信函多有模式可循,並不難寫。爲了幫助有志向學者,我們特在本書安排此一章節,除了教您書寫上述函件的祕訣外,亦提供一些留學小情報,讓您對留學有初步的認識。

學校類信函寫法

課業信函

假條是常見的學校類信函，內容宜簡短扼要，說明請假的**原因與天數**。若是病假可附上醫生的證明書，事假則應預先通知老師，請求批准。父母基於關心，會主動與師長溝通子女的問題。但詢問時，語氣宜謙卑，尊重老師的專業知識，請求指教。

推薦函（*Recommendation Letter*）

多數的老師皆樂意爲學生寫推薦函，然而面對衆多學生的請求，可能無暇親自執筆，只有讓學生先行擬稿，再作修改與簽名。因此學生在撰稿時，應模擬老師的口吻。推薦函不外是讚美，但也不宜誇大不實，最好能舉出實例來證明能力。

推薦函的長度以**一頁**爲佳，分三至四段書寫。每封推薦函最好能提出不同的優點，打字時也宜選用不同字體，才能顯出是由不同的老師所寫。

讀書計畫（*Plan of Study*）

讀書計畫在說明未來的學習方向，撰寫時應掌握以下要點：(1)**出國動機**，(2)**工作經驗**，(3)**計畫攻讀的領域**，(4)**申請該校的原因**，(5)**曾修過的相關課程**。讀書計畫在供評審委員作入學資格的參考，所以應積極表現。若有著作，可將之英譯附上。

請病假

September 3, 1998

Dear Sir,

Owing to a very bad cold, I am afraid I will not be able to attend school today. Furthermore my doctor advised me that I won't be able to resume my studies until next week. I have enclosed a signed certificate. I hope that you will forgive this unfortunate period of non-attendance.

Yours respectfully,

1998 年 9 月 3 日

親愛的老師：

　　由於重感冒，我今天恐怕無法上學。此外，醫生囑咐我要到下禮拜才能恢復上課。隨函附上醫師的簽字證明。希望您能原諒我這段期間的缺課。

敬上

** ***owing to*** 由於　resume〔rɪ'zjum〕*v.* 繼續
certificate〔sə'tɪfəkɪt〕*n.* 證明

請事假

March 15, 1998

Dear Ms. Connery,

I am afraid that John won't be able to attend school next Monday and Tuesday, as his presence is required at an important family event from Saturday to Tuesday.

As I don't want him to fall behind, I would be thankful if you could give John extra work to ensure he makes up for the missed assignments. I will make sure that he keeps up with his studies.

Yours sincerely,

Future Absence

1998 年 3 月 15 日

親愛的康納莉老師：

　　我很抱歉約翰下週一及週二都無法上學，因爲從週六至週二，家族中的一項重大事件，他都必須在場。

　　由於我不想讓他受落後之苦，不知您可否幫約翰出額外的功課，以確保他補回漏上的課。我一定會確實注意，讓約翰的功課跟得上。

敬上

　** keep up with 趕上

SUGGESTIONS ·············

　　由父母來請事假較具說服力，可請求老師出額外的作業讓孩子的進度不致落後，此外也應表示願負起督導的責任。

 與師長溝通

May 25, 1998

Dear Mr. Brown,

As you know, my son David has been in your class for the last two years and will soon graduate. Of course I am anxious about his future, and I have spoken to him about his future career and likely results in the final examinations.

As you should have a more realistic assessment than my son, I would ask for your evaluation. In your opinion, does he have a good chance of doing well? Do you think he has any particular talent? Could you suggest a profession for him? I am sorry about troubling you and I would appreciate your answer.

Yours sincerely,

Letter to a Teacher

1998 年 5 月 25 日

親愛的布朗先生：

　　小犬大衛過去兩年來，一直在您的班上就讀，很快就要畢業了。我當然很替他的前途操心，我也和他談過他的未來生涯，以及期末考試可能的結果。

　　您應該比小犬有更實際的評估，所以我想請問一下您的評量。在您看來，大衛可能考得理想嗎？您認為他有任何特殊才能嗎？您能建議一個適合他的行業嗎？很抱歉麻煩您，若能惠賜高見，自當不勝感激。

敬上

** anxious 〔ˈæŋ(k)ʃəs〕*adj.* 憂心的
realistic 〔ˌrɪəˈlɪstɪk〕*adj.* 實際的
assessment 〔əˈsɛsmənt〕*n.* 評估
in one's opinion 依某人看法

申請學校

July 10,1998

Dear Sir,

I wish to apply to pursue a Master's degree in Computer Science at your university, starting in the fall of 1999, and I would like you to send me the relevant application forms for admissions and financial support.

In 1995, I graduated from the Computer Science and Information Engineering Department of National Taiwan University, obtaining a B.S. degree. After military service from 1996 to 1997, I returned to the university as a teaching assistant, where I have been for the last year.

In the two tests required, I have scored 570 on the TOEFL, and 1750 on the GRE.

Sincerely yours,

Application

1998 年 7 月 10 日

敬啓者：

　　我想申請攻讀貴校 1999 年秋季班，資訊科學系的碩士學位，希望您能把有關研究所入學許可、及獎助學金的申請表格寄給我。

　　我 1995 年畢業於台大資訊工程系，拿到學士學位。從 1996 至 1997 服完兩年兵役之後，去年我回到學校當了一年助教。

　　閣下所要求的二項考試，我托福考 570 分，GRE 性向測驗 1750 分。

敬上

** pursue〔pəˊsu〕*v.* 繼續
　　B.S. 或 B.Sc. 是 Bachelor of Science 的縮寫

INFORMATION ·················

　　一旦決定留學志願學校，就可寫信到學校索取申請表與簡介，或以 RAM 表（Request for Application Material）代替寫信，三週內約可收到回覆。RAM 表格可向學術交流基金會購買。

　　托福測驗（Test of English as a Foreign Language，簡稱**TOEFL**），是赴英語系國家留學的學生，所必先通過的考試。**GRE** 測驗（Graduate Record Examination）是赴美、加研究所深造的資格考試，若欲攻讀商學，則考**GMAT**（Graduate Management Admission Test）。

 讀書計畫

Statement of Academic Objectives
by Chen Ping

I graduated from the Department of Computer Science and Information Engineering, National Taiwan University, in June 1995. After graduation I obtained a position at New Spring Computer Information Company, located in the Hsinchu Industrial Park, Taiwan. I have held this position until now.

In most data processing applications, the older methods of sorting and updating information are no longer adequate. With new technology providing faster machines and more complicated programs, our present systems have to be updated and improved to meet the requirements of our customers. Recognizing this fact I feel it is necessary to further my studies and so increase my knowledge in the field of data processing algorithms.

I hope to complete a Master's Degree in data processing and I believe that your university can help me fulfil my academic objectives.

Plan of Study

讀書計畫
陳平

　　我於一九九五年六月，自台灣大學資訊工程系畢業。畢業後，我進入台灣新竹工業園區的新春電腦資訊公司服務，直至今日。

　　在大多數資料處理的應用上，老舊的資料分類及更新的方法，已不再合宜。隨著新科技提供更快速的機器，以及更複雜的程式時，我們現有的系統必須更新改進，以符合顧客的需要。在體認到這個事實後，我感覺有必要繼續我的研究，以增進我在資料處理演算法這個領域的知識。

　　我希望能拿到資料處理的碩士學位，相信貴校能助我達成學術目標。

　　**　academic〔͵ækə'dɛmɪk〕*adj.* 學術的
　　objective〔əb'dʒɛktɪv〕*n.* 目標
　　application〔͵æplə'keʃən〕*n.* 應用
　　sort〔sɔrt〕*v.* 分類　update〔'ʌp͵det〕*v.* 更新
　　algorithm〔'ælgə͵rɪðm̩〕*n.*（電腦）演算法

推薦函

September 28, 1998

Dear Sir,

It is with great pleasure that I am writing on behalf of my student, Ms. Chen Hsiao Li. Ms. Chen attended National Taiwan University from 1990 to 1994, graduating from the Department of Foreign Languages and Literature.

I taught *Introduction to Linguistics* to Ms. Chen in her second year. During that time I was impressed by her intelligence and her eagerness to learn. As well as being a talented student, her modesty, pleasing personality and willingness to help made her popular with both the staff and her fellow students. Her work has indicated a mature attitude and critical skills. Her command of English is excellent and she was ranked 27th in a class of 130 students.

Ms. Chen has declared a firm desire to pursue graduate study at your university. I recommend her wholeheartedly and believe she will be an outstanding graduate student. Your careful consideration of her application would be highly appreciated.

Yours Sincerely,

Professor
Dept. of Foreign Languages
and Literature
National Taiwan University

Recommendation

1998 年 9 月 28 日

敬啓者：

　　我很高興能有機會寫信推薦我的學生陳小莉。陳小姐於 1990－1994 年間就讀於台灣大學，畢業於外國語文學系。

　　我在陳小姐大二時，教授她「語言學概論」。那時，我就對她的聰穎及求知慾，留下了深刻的印象。除了資賦優異之外，陳小姐虛懷若谷、個性宜人、且熱心助人，使得她在師長及同學間的人緣都非常好。她的功課顯示出她成熟的態度，以及評判的技巧。她的英文造詣也極爲優越，在全班一百三十名同學中，她名列二十七。

　　陳小姐已表達了攻讀貴校研究所的強烈欲望。我由衷地推薦她，相信她會是一名傑出的研究生。閣下若能仔細考慮其申請，自當不勝感激。

敬上
國立台灣大學外國語文學系教授

** *on behalf of* 代表
　　linguistics〔lɪŋ'gwɪstɪks〕*n.* 語言學
　　modesty〔'madəstɪ〕*n.* 謙遜
　　staff〔stæf〕*n.* 單位人員（集合稱）
　　declare〔dɪ'klɛr〕*v.* 聲明
　　wholehearted〔'hol'hartɪd〕*adj.* 熱誠的

 決定入學

April 30，1998

Dear Mr. Buchanan,

Thank you for your letter dated April 12th informing me that I have been accepted as a student for the 1998 academic year.

Needless to say I am very happy and flattered, and I do plan to attend.

By the end of this week I will have sent you the information you requested concerning my scholarship and accommodation needs.

Yours sincerely,

Acceptance

1998 年 4 月 30 日

親愛的 布肯納先生：

　謝謝您 4 月 12 日的來信，通知我已獲准於 1998 學年度入學。

　我的喜悅自是不在話下，我決定要入學。

　在這個禮拜之前，我會將您要求的資料寄給您，其中包括了我所需要的獎學金及住宿。

敬上

** scholarship〔'skɑləˌʃɪp〕*n.* 獎學金
accommodation〔əˌkɑməˈdeʃən〕*n.* 住宿

INFORMATION ··············

　若決定入學，需聯絡該校的留學生管理部門，並同時辦理相關事宜，如入學手續、投保、住宿等。

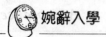 婉辭入學

April 30, 1998

Dear Mr. Buchanan,

Thank you for your letter of April 12th informing me that I have been accepted as a student for the 1998 academic year.

Despite being grateful for your acceptance of my application, I am afraid I am unable to attend Western Vermont College, as I have already made other arrangements for my further education. Enclosed is the I-20 form which I am returning.

Yours sincerely,

Rejection

1998年4月30日

親愛的布肯納先生：

　　謝謝您4月12日的來函，通知我已獲准於1998學年度入學。

　　雖然很感激您接受我的申請，但是我恐怕無法進入西佛蒙特學院就讀，因為我已為我的深造做了其他規劃，隨信並附上我退還的入學許可證。

敬上

INFORMATION ·················

　　若獲准入學，學校會寄上入學許可證，即 **I-20**，「**I**」表示移民歸化局（Immigration and Naturalization Service）。假使不想就讀該校，或想延緩入學時間，都需寄回 I-20 。

延期入學

May 20, 1998

Dear Sir,

Due to unforseen circumstances, I will not be able to enroll this coming semester. Please change my date of entry to the Fall of 2000. Enclosed in this letter is the I-20 form, which I am returning.

I apologize for the inconvenience caused.

Yours sincerely,

1998 年 5 月 20 日

敬啓者：

由於發生些始料未及的事，使我這學期無法註冊入學。請將我的入學日期改成二〇〇〇年秋天。隨函附上的，是我退還給您的入學許可證。

我對我所引起的不便深深致歉。

敬上

** enroll〔ɪnˈrol〕*v.* 註冊　semester〔səˈmɛstə〕*n.* 學期

簽證機構

◆ American Institute in Taiwan, Taipei　美國在台協會台北辦事處
　　　Add: 7, Lane 134, Hsinyi Rd., Sec. 3, Taipei
　　　　　　台北市信義路三段 134 巷 7 號
　　　Tel: (02)709-2000　　　　　Fax: (02)702-7675

◆ American Institute in Taiwan, Kaohsiung　美國在台協會高雄分處
　　　Add: 5F, 2 Chungcheng 3rd Rd., Kaohsiung
　　　　　　高雄市中正三路 2 號 5 樓
　　　Tel: (07)224-0154　　　　　Fax: (07)223-8237

◆ British Trade and Cultural Office　英國貿易文化辦事處
　　　Add: 9F, 99 Jen-ai Rd., Sec2., Taipei
　　　　　　台北市仁愛路二段 99 號 9 樓
　　　Tel: (02)322-4242, 322-3235　　　　Fax: (02)394-8673

◆ Australian Commerce and Industry Office　澳大利亞商工辦事處
　　　Add: Rm.2605, 333 Keelung Rd., Sec.1, Taipei
　　　　　　台北市基隆路一段 333 號 2605 室
　　　Tel: (02)722-0772　　　　　Fax: (02)757-6040

◆ Canadian Trade Office in Taipei　加拿大駐台北貿易辦事處
　　　Add: 13F, 365 Fuhsing N. Rd., Taipei
　　　　　　台北市復興北路 365 號 13 樓
　　　Tel: (02)713-7268　　　　　Fax: (02)712-7244

◆ The Institute for Trade and Investment of Ireland
　　愛爾蘭投資貿易促進會
　　　Add: Rm.7B-09, 5 Hsinyi Rd., Sec.5, Taipei
　　　　　　台北市信義路五段 5 號 7B-09 室
　　　Tel: (02)725-1691　　　　　Fax: (02)725-1653

◆ New Zealand Commerce and Industry Office　紐西蘭商工辦事處
　　　Add: Suite 2501, 25F, 333 Keelung Rd., Sec.1, Taipei
　　　　　　台北市基隆路一段 333 號 25 樓 2501 室
　　　Tel: (02)757-7060　　　　　Fax: (02)757-6973

留學資料查詢機構

♥ **Anglo-Taiwan Education Center** 英國教育中心

　　Add: 7F, 99 Jen-ai Rd., Sec. 2, Taipei
　　　　台北市仁愛路二段 99 號 7 樓
　　Tel: (02)396-2238　　　　Fax: (02)341-5749

♥ **Foundation for Scholarly Exchange / Fulbright Foundation**
　學術交流基金會

　　Add: 2F, 1-A, Chuanchow St., Taipei
　　　　台北市泉州街 1-A 號 2 樓
　　Tel: (02)332-8188　　　　Fax: (02)332-5445

♥ **American Cultural Center Library** 美國文化中心圖書館

　　Add: 54 Nanhai Rd., Taipei
　　　　台北市南海路 54 號
　　Tel: (02)305-2382　　　　Fax: (02)305-6757

♥ **IDP Education Australia / Australian Education Center**
　澳洲教育中心

　　Suite 2602, 26F, International Trade Building,
　　333 Keelung Rd., Sec. 1, Taipei
　　　　台北市基隆路一段 333 號國貿大樓 26 樓 2602 室
　　Tel: (02)757-6334　　　　Fax: (02)757-6489

♥ **The Language Training and Testing Center** 語言訓練測驗中心

　　Add: 170 Hsin-hai Rd., Sec. 2, Taipei 106
　　　　P.O. Box 23-41, Taipei, Taiwan
　　　　台北市辛亥路 2 段 170 號
　　Tel: (02)362-6045

♥ 教育部國際文教處留學生服務中心及留學生圖書館

　　Add: 1F, 100 Aikwo E. Rd., Taipei
　　　　台北市愛國東路 100 號 1F
　　Tel: (02)397-0773　　　　Fax: (02)322-5189

貿易書信

CHAPTER 5

　　台灣以一蕞爾小島之姿，卻創造了舉世震驚的經濟奇蹟，賺取外匯存底最多的出口貿易，實當居首功。由於美國是我傾銷產品的一大市場，再加上英語是國際語言，因此熟悉貿易英語將是經營外貿的基礎。為了讓初學者對貿易英語有所認識，本章將貿易過程大致分為數個階段，從申請交易、推銷產品、金錢交涉、到裝運、索賠、理賠等，都有簡潔基礎的介紹，在每一貿易步驟後，並附有書信實例以資參考學習。知己知彼，百戰百勝，要想做個成功的外貿人才，對貿易英語可要瞭若指掌！

Unit 1 ► 商業書信常識

商業書信結構

在第一章部份，我們已介紹過一般書信的結構。商業書信中，除前述的基本架構，還添加一些項目以利作業：

- **信頭**（Letterhead）：功能和寄信人住址（Heading）相同，通常都已印在公司的專用信箋上。

- **檔案號碼**（File Reference）：為了方便處理與查詢，在信件上會打上編號，如 Reference：No.100

- **日期**（Date Line）：發信的日期

- **特定收信人**（Attention Line）：指定收信人的姓名及職稱。寫法是 attention 後面加上人名，如：ATTENTION Mr. John Philips, Attention Mr. John Philips, Attention：Mr. John Philips。

- **主題**（Subject Matter）：寫在正文之前，方便收信人一目瞭然信件的大意，可全用大寫或加底線使之醒目。

- **責任記號**（Reference Initials）：信件負責人與打字員的姓名縮寫。負責人的名字用大寫，打字員用小寫，可以斜線或冒號隔開，如：PE/ch 或 PE：ch。

- **附件**（Enclosure）：標明隨信附寄的文件。若附件不只一份，則在 Enclosure 後加上數目，如：Enclosures（3）。

- **影本**（Carbon Copy Notation）：同樣的書信若有副本寄給其他公司或單位，需在最後加上 cc：**商號名稱**的註明，如 cc：Learning Co. Ltd.

商業書信格式

常見的商業書信格式有三種：

■ **齊頭式**（Block Style）：除了印在信紙上的信頭（Letterhead）外，其餘的項目全都靠左端書寫。

■ **折衷式**（Modified Block Style）：將日期、結尾謙辭、署名用縮排，其餘全對齊左端書寫。

■ **折衷段落縮排式**（Modified Block Style with Indented Paragraph）：正文的每段開頭都向內縮排五個字左右，日期、結尾謙辭、署名和折衷式相同，也要縮排。

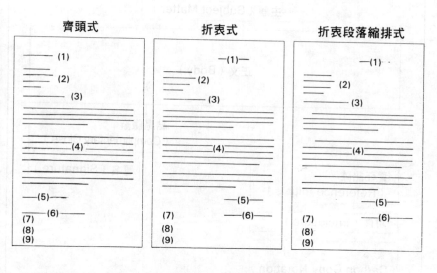

(1) 日期　　　　(2) 收信人姓名地址　　(3) 稱謂
(4) 正文　　　　(5) 結尾謙辭　　　　　(6) 署名
(7) 責任記號　　(8) 附件　　　　　　　(9) 影本

信頭（Letterhead）

檔案號碼
（File Reference）

日期（Date Line）

收信人住址
（Inside Address）

特定收信人
（Attention Line）

稱謂（Salutation）

主題（Subject Matter）

正文（Body）

結尾謙辭
（Complimentary Close）

署名（Signature）

責任記號
（Reference Initials）

附件（Enclosure）

影本
（Carbon Copy Notation）

（折衷式商業書信）

Pioneer Software Company
54 Tunhwa South Rd., Sec. 2
Taipei, Taiwan, R.O.C.
Tel: 886-2-704-5525   FAX: 886-2-707-9095

Reference: No. 101
March 5, 1998

Computer Emporium
1290 Lake Shore Drive
Chicago, IL 51231
U.S.A.

ATTENTION: Mr. Alfred Sloan

Gentlemen:

Offer of Product

I was very happy to receive your reply and hear that your sales staff are happy with our latest software.

For an order of 400 units the price is $55.00 per unit, payment by T/T. On confirmation of your payment, delivery will be done immediately.

To expedite delivery please let us know the address of your forwarder.

Yours sincerely,

Kathy Wu

Kathy Wu
Sales Manager

KW/sc
Enclosure (2)
CC: Macrosoft Computer Company

（折衷式商業書信）

Unit 2 ▶ 開發‧推銷‧詢價

開發（*Proposal of Business*）

　　開發客戶是交易中最重要的課題。貿易對象的好壞，直接影響營運結果，因此，在挑選客戶時需格外謹愼。交易的對象可透過工商名册（ Kelley's Directory ）、業界刊物、專業雜誌的廣告，以及展覽會、政府機關等途徑來尋獲。

　　交易提案可**寄給多家公司**，以增加成功的機率。內容要先提及獲悉對方的過程，然後簡略地自我介紹，說明與我方交易的好處，可獲得的利潤。最好能附上目錄、價目表等資料，供對方參考。結尾部份要表達期盼回覆的心情，讓對方了解你的誠意。

推銷（*Sales*）

　　所謂推銷是利用各種機會，積極展開銷售的意思。推銷的時機頗多，諸如發售新產品、擴充營運、清倉、設立分公司等，都是不可錯失的良機。

　　推銷不宜沿用舊有的交易模式，應該採取**大膽、積極**的態度。推銷信函需運用新鮮、有力的言辭，方能擄獲對方的心。在策略上，可以利用客觀事實、實驗數據，強調商品的品質，或是以感性的方式，打動對方的意志。

詢價（*Inquiry*）

詢價是買方向賣方詢問欲購商品的價格，以及交易的條件。詢問函可單純索取目錄、樣品，或是明確指出欲購商品的名稱、預訂數量、裝貨日期等具體交易。

內容開頭應敘述如何得知對方，若彼此曾有過交易，可直接切入主題，進行查詢。結尾部份可暗示成交的可能性，誘使對方儘速回覆。

回覆詢價（*Reply to Inquiry*）

詢價是成交的預兆，收到詢問函後，需**立即回覆**，因為買方可能同時詢問多家廠商，儘早回覆可取得優勢。交易條件不能隨性所訂，應強調自己的特性、優點、與價格的合理，才能爭取買方的訂單。

對於買方詢問的事項，要全部回答，切勿閃爍其辭。若無法立即答覆，應先告知，待一切準備周全後，再另行通知。

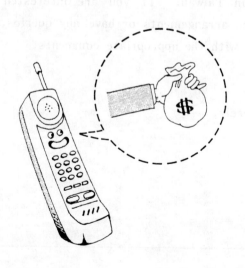

申請交易

Dear Sir,

Our company has noticed the increasing popularity of your latest product and its increasing market share. We are one of the largest importers in Taiwan with an extensive sales staff who are all fluent in English, Mandarin, and Taiwanese. We have a local distribution network all over the island and so can guarantee prompt delivery of your product from any port of entry.

We believe we can be of great assistance in helping you achieve a greater share of the Taiwanese market and we are very interested in representing you in Taiwan. If you are interested in any future arrangements or have any queries, please reply with the appropriate comments.

Sincerely,

Proposal of Business

敬啓者:

敝公司注意到貴公司最新的產品,愈來愈受歡迎,且市場佔有率愈來愈高。我們是台灣最大的進口商之一,有衆多精通英、國、台語的推銷員。我們在台灣全島都有分佈網,所以可保證,貴產品無論從任何港口進貨,都能夠迅速運送。

我們自信對您在拓展台灣市場上,能有莫大的助益。我們也非常願意做為您在台的代理商。如果您對未來的籌備也感興趣,或有任何的疑問,請不吝賜教。

敬上

** distribution〔͵dɪstrə'bjuʃən〕*n.* 分佈
　　guarantee〔͵gærən'ti〕*v.* 保證
　　represent〔͵rɛprɪ'zɛnt〕*v.* 代表
　　query〔'kwɪrɪ〕*n.* 疑問

推銷產品

Dear Mr. Wu,

We are most pleased to introduce you to our latest software, a major improvement over our previous version, which as you know is quite popular in the market. From monitoring the Internet as well as direct communication with our customers, our engineers have been able to determine the bugs in the previous software version and correct them, as well as add new features.

We are confident of the success of our latest software, and since you have been one of our best distributors in Asia, we would like to offer you a 10% discount for the first shipment. Furthermore, we will take back your remaining unsold copies of the previous version.

Looking forward to continued mutual success in the market,

Introduction to Product

吳先生：

　　很高興能為您介紹敝公司最新的軟體。誠如您所知，前一版的軟體在市場上大受歡迎，而我們這次的版本更是大有改進。從國際網際網路的偵測，以及與顧客的直接溝通，我們的工程師已經找出舊版的毛病，並且加以修正，此外也加入新的功能。

　　我們對新版的軟體深具信心。由於您是敝公司在亞洲的優良經銷商，我們願意在第一次裝運時，提供九折的優待。此外，我們也會收回您未售出的舊版存貨。

　　期盼再度合作大發利市。

** monitor〔ˈmɑnətɚ〕*v.* 監視，電腦螢幕也稱作monitor
　　 Internet 國際網際網路
　　 bug〔bʌg〕*n.* 機器的缺點
　　 distributor〔dɪˈstrɪbjətɚ〕*n.* 經銷商

查詢

Dear Ms. Johnson,

Until recently our company has concentrated mostly on mainframes and PCs, with software being a minor part of our business. However we have decided to branch out into software, and have been very impressed by your popular software. Until now we have dealt with you through a middleman, but we believe we can achieve a substantial increase in sales if we deal directly with you, and if we can have a discount for large quantity orders.

We would appreciate it if you could reply with your best price quotes.

Looking forward to your reply and increasing business,

Inquiry

強森小姐：

　　直到最近，敝公司一直都將大部分重心放在大型主機與個人電腦上，而軟體只佔業務的一小部分。然而，我們已決定要擴大軟體業務的規模，也對廣爲流行的貴產品印象深刻。至今，我們已透過中間商與您進行交易。但是我們相信，若能與您直接交易，並以大量訂購來得到折扣，我們將可在銷售上達到更顯著的成長。

　　若能將您最優待的報價予以告知，我們會很感激的。敬候佳音並祝業務蒸蒸日上。

** mainframe 〔'men,frem〕 *n.* 大型主機
　　PC 是 personal computer（個人電腦）的縮寫
　　branch out 擴充
　　middleman 〔'mɪdḷ,mæn〕 *n.* 居間人
　　substantial 〔səb'stænʃəl〕 *adj.* 相當的
　　quote 〔kwot〕 *n.* 報價

 **答覆查詢**

Dear Mr. Hsieh,

I was very interested to hear of your plans to expand into software sales. We have previously noticed your company's success and, given your excellent sales of computer hardware and accessaries, we believe you will do equally well in the field of software sales.

Accompanying this letter you will find a copy of our latest software for your evaluation. If you are satisfied with this product, we are ready to begin immediate shipment. For bulk orders we are prepared to offer a 5％ discount for orders over 500 units and 10％ for orders of 1,000 units.

Please contact us with any comments and the appropriate details.

Yours sincerely,

Reply to Inquiry

謝先生：

聽到您有意拓展軟體銷售，令我非常感興趣。我們已注意到貴公司的成功，再加上您在電腦硬體及配件的銷售佳績，相信您在軟體銷售方面，也同樣能勝任愉快。

隨函附上我們最新的軟體，供作參考。若您對該產品滿意的話，我們已準備好可立即開始出貨。大量訂購逾五百套，我們可提供九五折、逾一千套九折優待。

請與我們聯絡，並祈不吝賜教。

敬上

** accessary〔æk'sɛsərɪ〕*n.* 附件（亦作 accessory）
bulk〔bʌlk〕*n.* 大量

Unit 3 報價・還價

報價 (*Offer*)

　　報價是賣方針對買方提出的交易內容，所給予的具體承諾，其中包含交易條件、商品內容、數量、價格、裝運期等。一般報價都由賣方提出，稱為賣方報價（Seller's Offer）或銷售報價（Selling Offer），若由買方提出，則稱為出價（Bid）。常見的報價可分幾類：

■ **確定報價**（Firm Offer）：賣方所提的報價，在承諾期限內不變，亦不受市價影響，但一超過期限，報價自動失效。

■ **經確認有效報價**（Offer Subject to Confirmation）：賣方所提的報價，雖經買方承諾，但仍不算正式契約，必須由買方書面確認後才生效。

■ **有權先售報價**（Offer Subject to Prior Sale, Offer Subject to Being Unsold）：賣方對數個買主進行報價，以先到先售為原則，隨著貨物售盡，報價也告失效。

　　報價函除說明報價的種類、產品價格與銷售條件，也要極力推銷交易的好處，誘使買方訂購。

還價 (*Counter Offer*)

　　賣方所提的報價，很少會被買方照單全收，雙方會經過多次協調與修改，此即還價。一旦買方提出還價，原有的報價即失效。為爭取時效，還價通常以電報或傳真進行，在書寫上，應先感謝賣方的報價，然後提出不合理的內容，與希望的條件，最後請對方及早回覆。

承諾（*Acceptance*）

當買賣雙方對交易條件達成協議，發出完全的承諾（Absolute Acceptance），便可確立交易關係訂定契約。此時買方需擬好**購買確認書**（Purchase Note），賣方也需擬定**銷售確認書**（Sales Note），彼此交予對方審查。

也可由買方下**訂單**（Order），送交賣方審查，再由賣方寄**訂單確認書**（Confirmation of Order）給買方，經確認無誤，由買方在兩份契約上簽名，保留正本，將副本寄還給賣方。

‖‖‖‖‖‖‖ 商用英文略語(票據、匯款) ‖‖‖‖‖‖‖

B/C＝bill for collection 託收票據

B/D, B.D.＝bank draft 銀行匯票；bill discounted 貼現票據

B/E, b.e.＝bill of exchange 匯票

B/P, b.p., B.P.＝bills payable 應付匯票；bill purchased 買入匯票

B/R, b.r.＝bills receivable 應收票據

D.D., D/D＝demand draft 即期匯票；documentary draft 跟單匯票

dft.＝draft 匯票

M.O.＝money order (郵局) 匯票

M/T＝mail transfer 信匯

T.M.O.＝telegraphic money order 電報匯款

T.T., T/T＝telegraphic transfer 電匯

P/N＝promissory note 本票；期票

S.D., S/D＝sight draft 即期匯票

T/A＝trade acceptance 商業承兌匯票

報價

Dear Mr. Hsieh,

I was very happy to receive your reply and hear that your sales staff are happy with our latest software.

For an order of 500 units the price is 50.00 per unit, payment by T/T. On confirmation of your payment, delivery will be done immediately.

To expedite delivery please let us know the address of your forwarder.

Yours sincerely,

Offer

謝先生：

很高興收到您的回覆，並得知您的營業人員對我們最新的軟體都很滿意。

若訂購500套的話，單價是50元，以電匯方式付款，一旦您的付款被確認，就會馬上出貨。

為了便利運送起見，請告知我們您承運公司的地址。

敬上

** T/T 是 telegraphic transfer（電匯）的縮寫
confirmation〔͵kɑnfəˈmeʃən〕*n.* 確認
expedite〔ˈɛkspɪ͵daɪt〕*v.* 加速
forwarder〔ˈfɔrwɚdɚ〕*n.* 運輸者

買方還價

Dear Ms. Johnson,

Thank you for your prompt reply and quote. Your software was very impressive indeed, and more than fulfilled our expectations.

As we have already begun to receive inquiries, we would like to start ordering your new version as soon as possible. However, I would like to discuss the issue of the price. I am afraid that at $50.00 per unit for 500 units, we will not be able to offer a competitive price and so achieve the sales we hoped for. As we are certain we can order enough software to compensate for a lower price, please let me know if there is any possibility of a reduction in price.

I am looking forward to your reply.

Sincerely yours,

Counter Offer

強森小姐：

　　謝謝您馬上回覆並寄來報價表。貴公司的軟體的確令人印象深刻，超出我們預期的水準。

　　由於我們已接到詢問，因此我們想儘快向貴公司訂購，然而，在價格方面還有待商榷。若以每套 50 元承購500 套，我們將無法提供有競爭力的價格，以達到預期的銷售量。我們確信可以訂購足夠的軟體，以彌補低價的差額，若您可以再降價，請通知我方。

　　期盼您的回音。

敬上

**　inquiry〔 ɪnˋkwaɪrɪ 〕*n.* 詢問 (亦作 enquiry)
　　competitive〔 kəmˋpɛtətɪv 〕*adj.* 有競爭力的
　　compensate〔 ˋkɑmpən͵set 〕*v.* 賠償
　　reduction〔 rɪˋdʌkʃən 〕*n.* 降低

賣方還價

Dear Mr. Hsieh,

Following your prompt reply I have raised the issue with my superiors. We believe that you are a customer with a great deal of potential, and since we are eager to do business with you, we have agreed to make you a better offer. The lowest price we can give you is $23.50 per unit. This is the price we only offer to our best customers.

If this is appropriate, please reply with your confirmation and the address of your forwarder. All payments are to be made via our bank, First Bank of California.

Yours sincerely,

Counter Offer

謝先生：

依照您的回函，我已向主管提出問題。我們深信貴公司
有極大的潛力，也極欲與您合作，所以我們願意提供貴
方更優惠的價格。我們所能出的最低價錢是每套23.5
元，這只提供給最佳的顧客。

如果價錢合理，請回函確認，並告知我們貴方承運公司
的地址。所有款項請交付第一加州銀行。

敬上

**　superior〔səˈpɪrɪə〕*n.* 上司
　　via〔ˈvaɪə〕*prep.* 經由

承諾

Dear Ms. Johnson,

Thank you for your prompt reply. Your latest price quote is acceptable and I have already started a training program on selling your software. Our sales staff are all excited about selling your software and we expect very good sales results.

We would like to put in an initial order for 500 units. Our accounts department has been instructed to transfer the appropriate funds to your bank. Our forwarder is Mr. Frank Smith of Duke Express.

We look forward to a successful business relationship with your company.

Sincerely,

Acceptance

強森小姐：

感謝您立即的回覆。我接受您最新的報價，並已針對銷售貴軟體，展開了一套訓練計畫。我們的業務員對能銷售貴軟體，都感到無比興奮，我們期盼著銷售佳績。

第一次我們想先訂 500 套。我們已告知會計部門，將該筆專款轉入您的銀行帳戶。我們的承運人是廸爵快遞的法蘭克‧史密斯先生。

預祝彼此合作愉快，事業順利成功。

敬上

** ***put in*** 提出
　initial〔ɪˋnɪʃəl〕*adj.* 開始的
　instruct〔ɪnˋstrʌkt〕*v.* 指示
　fund〔fʌnd〕*n.* 專款

Unit 4 ▶ 訂單·裝運·索賠

訂單 (*Order*)

　　前一單元提到，交易的達成須經過買賣雙方多次報價、還價，直到達成協議為止。但是買方也可單憑賣方所寄的樣品（Sample）、目錄（Catalogue）、價目表（Price List）等，直接發出訂單（Order Sheet）。若賣方願意接受訂購，買賣契約即告成立。買方寄出訂單或**購買確認書**（Purchase Note）向賣方做訂貨的保證；而賣方也發出**訂購確認書**（Confirmation of Order, Acknowledgement of Order）或**銷售確認書**（Sales Notes），確認已成立的買賣契約。

　　在訂貨方面，買方可使用自製的訂購單（Order Sheet, Order Form），在表格上打出各項目，或是採用訂購函（Order Letter）的方式，在信文中條列訂購內容，如商品細目、交貨期、數量、價格等條件。

裝運通知 (*Shipping Advice*)

　　待貨物完成裝船後，賣方應立刻以電報或傳真，拍發裝運通知（Shipping Advice）給買方，爾後再以書信確認。裝運通知不僅告知買方裝運完成，亦有提醒籌措貨款、訂定銷售計畫的作用。

　　裝運通知函除對電報或傳真的內容加以確認，亦應寫明貨物品名、數量、船名、裝船日期或開航日期、抵達日期、以及跟單滙票的處理情形，最後再申希望貨物安全抵達之意。

索賠（*Making a Claim*）

當貨物安全抵達買方手中，所有程序也都按照合約履行，該項交易便可告一段落。其中若發生變故，買方可依權利提出索賠。索賠包括因不可抗拒因素產生的**運輸索賠**（ Transportation Claim ）、**保險索賠**（ Insurance Claim ），以及賣方疏失的**貿易索賠**（ Trade Claim ），如產品不良、破損、延遲交貨等因素。

運輸、保險的問題可逕向運輸公司或保險公司索賠，極少有通信的必要，真正需要溝通的是貿易索賠。抱怨、請求賠償時，要正確、清楚的陳述事實，避免指責或激烈的言辭，否則會收到反效果。

收到索賠的一方，應先聽取對方陳述，然後查明真相。若賣方有錯，應坦誠並具體提出解決方法，推卸責任將會使往後的交易難以進行。如果錯不在己，應舉出實證，讓對方信服。

買賣雙方若無法和解（Compromise），則需藉調停（Mediation）、仲裁（Arbitration）、甚至訴訟（Litigation）等方式來解決。

商用英文略語(條狀、証明書)

C/O = certificate of origin
原產地證明書

D/A = documents against
acceptance 承兌交單

D/P = documents against
payment 付款交單

ED = export declaration
出口申報書

I.O.U. = I owe you 借條

I/P = insurance policy 保險單

L/C = letter of credit 信用狀

L/G = letter of guarantee 保證書

L/H = letter of hypothecation
質押證書

L/I = letter of indemnity
賠償保證書

R.O. = remittance order
匯款委託書

訂貨

Dear Mr. Emerson,

We import large amounts of fruit from Australia, but, unfortunately our original supplier has entered bankruptcy proceedings, leaving us uncertain of a continued supply.

We wish to place an order for 5,000 kilograms of kiwi fruit to be delivered by sea via the Port of Brisbane as with our previous supplier.

If you can meet this order, please let us know as soon as possible.

Yours sincerely,

Making an Order

愛默森先生：

我們從澳洲進口大量的水果，但是，很不幸地，我們原本的供應商已進入了宣告破產的訴訟程序，使我們無法確定能否繼續獲得供應。

我們想要訂購 5000 公斤的奇異果，並請如我們先前的廠商一樣，經由布里斯本以海運送貨。

如果你能接下這張訂單，請儘速給我們回覆。

敬上

** supplier〔səˈplaɪɚ〕*n.* 供應者
   bankruptcy〔ˈbæŋkrʌptsɪ〕*n.* 破產
   proceedings〔prəˈsidɪŋz〕*n. pl.* 訴訟程序
   kiwi fruit 奇異果
   Brisbane〔ˈbrɪzbən〕*n.* 布里斯本（澳洲東岸之海港城市，為 Queensland 之首府）

接受訂單

Dear Mr. Wang,

I was pleased to receive your letter. We would be glad to provide for your order of 5,000 kilograms of kiwi fruit. We already have extensive experience delivering fruit to Yokohama and Seoul and have had many satisfied customers in the Far East region.

As soon as the appropriate funds are transfered to our bank in Taipei, we will immediately arrange the shipment.

Yours sincerely,

Accepting an Order

王先生：

很高興收到你的信。我們很樂意提供您 5000 公斤的奇異果。對於運送水果到橫濱和漢城，我們已有很廣泛的經驗。在遠東一帶，也有許多對我們深表滿意的客戶。

一旦數額正確的專款滙入我們在台北的銀行戶頭，我們就會馬上安排運送事宜。

敬上

** Yokohama〔͵jokoˈhɑmə〕*n.* 橫濱
　 Seoul〔sol〕*n.* 漢城
　 region〔ˈridʒən〕*n.* 區域

拒絕訂單

Dear Mr. Wang,

I was very pleased to receive your order of 5,000 kilograms of kiwi fruit, but I am afraid I cannot meet your order at this time. I already have a large customer in Yokohama and have no excess stock.

However, I believe that apples might fulfill your requirements. I have already made preliminary inquiries and I am sure that 5,000 kilograms can be supplied. If you are interested, please contact me.

Sincerely,

Declining an Order

王先生：

我很高興能接到您 5000 公斤奇異果的訂購，不過我這次恐怕無法滿足您訂購的需求。我已接下了橫濱一名大客戶，沒有多餘的存貨了。

然而蘋果可能可以符合您的需求。我已經初步查詢了一下，確定我可以供應 5000 公斤的蘋果。如果您有興趣的話，請和我聯絡。

敬上

** excess〔ɪk'sɛs〕*adj.* 多額的
stock〔stɑk〕*n.* 存貨
preliminary〔prɪ'lɪmə,nɛrɪ〕*adj.* 先前的

 裝運通知

Dear Mr. Wang,

I would like to confirm the departure of 5,000 kilograms of kiwi fruit on M/S Pioneer from the Port of Brisbane. They are scheduled to arrive at Keelung on January 15th.

The cargo has been insured by Fortune's of Brisbane and on board is the appropriate packing information for your agent upon arrival in Taiwan.

If there is any problem with the transportation of the shipment or the quality of the fruit, please let me know as soon as possible.

Sincerely,

Shipping Advice

王先生：

我想向您確認，5000 公斤的奇異果已從布里斯本由先鋒號運出，預定一月十五日抵達基隆。

貨物已由布里斯本的富星公司保險，船上的正確包裝處理，待船隻抵達台灣，提供給貴方的代理商。

如果對貨物的裝載及運送，或是水果的品質有任何問題，請儘快通知我。

敬上

** departure〔dɪˈpartʃə〕 *n.* 出發
  cargo〔ˈkɑrgo〕 *n.* 貨物
  insure〔ɪnˈʃʊr〕 *v.* 保險
  transportation〔ˌtrænspəˈteʃən〕 *n.* 運輸
  M/S 為 Motor Ship（馬達船）的縮寫，通常在船名前會標上 M/V（Motor Vessel）或 M/S 等船種名稱。不標明時，只要在船名前加上定冠詞 the 即可。

索賠

Dear Mr. Emerson,

Your shipment of 5,000 kilograms of kiwi fruit was delivered on time and the majority of the contents were received in good condition.

Unfortunately, some 30 crates spoiled during the voyage and are now useless to us. Therefore we would like to ask that you send an additional 30 crates, free of charge, in your next shipment.

Sincerely,

** crate〔kret〕*n.* 木條板箱
voyage〔'vɔɪ·ɪdʒ〕*n.* 航行

Making a Claim

愛默森先生：

您裝載的 5000 公斤奇異果已準時運達，大部份的品質都良好。

然而很不幸地，有 30 箱在運送途中爛掉，現在對我們來說是無用了。所以，我想要求您在下回運送時，免費多寄送 30 箱。

敬上

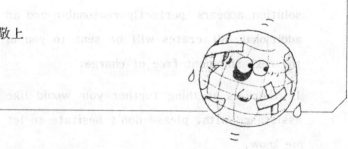

❀ 貿易索賠原因

Inferior Quality 品質不良	Different Quality 品質有異
Bad Package 包裝不良	Breakage 破損
Shortage 裝運不足	Different Shipment 裝運有異
Delayed Shipment 延遲裝運	Illegal Shipment 違法裝運
Breach of Contract 未履行契約	Cancellation 解約

理賠

Dear Mr. Wang,

Thank you for your letter. I am pleased to hear that you are satisfied with the quality and promptness of the shipment.

As to the 30 crates that did not survive, given the hot and humid weather, those sorts of losses are to be expected. Your proposed solution appears perfectly reasonable and an additional 30 crates will be sent to you in the next shipment free of charge.

If there is anything further you would like assistance with, please don't hesitate to let me know.

Sincerely yours,

Adjusting a Claim

王先生：

謝謝您的來信。我很高興聽到您對我們運送貨物的品質及效率感到滿意。

關於有 30 箱水果爛掉，我想在炎熱潮溼的天氣下，那種損害是難免的。您所提的解決之道非常合理，額外的 30 箱會在下次運送時，免費寄達給您。

如果您還有任何事需要協助的話，請儘管通知我。

敬上

** survive〔səˈvaɪv〕*v.* 存留
humid〔ˈhjumɪd〕*adj.* 潮溼的

常用商用英文略語（付款、保險）……

✦ 付款交貨

A/S, a/s = after sight 見票後
（…天付款）

C.A.D. = cash against documents
憑單付現

C.B.D. = cash before delivery
付現後交貨

C&D = collection & delivery
收款發貨

C&F, c.f. = cost and freight
運費在內價

C&I = cost and insurance 保險費
在內價

C.I.F. = cost, insurance and freight
保險費、運費在內價

C.I.F.&C. = cost, insurance, freight
and commission 保險費、運費、佣
金在內價

C.I.F.&I. = cost, insurance, freight
and interest 保險費、運費、利息
在內價

C.I.F.C.&I. = cost, insurance, freight,
commission and interest 保險費、
運費、佣金、利息在內價

C.O.D. = cash on delivery 貨到付現

c.o.s. = cash on shipment 裝船付款

C.W.O. = cash with order 訂貨付現

F.A.S. = free alongside ship
船邊交貨價

F/D = free docks 碼頭交貨

f.f.a. = free from alongside 船邊交
貨（此後運費買主自理）

F.I.O. = free in and out 運費不包括
裝卸費

F.O.B. = free on board 船上交貨價

✦ 保險・賠償

A.A.R. = against all risks 擔保全險

A.R., a.r. = all risks 全險

F.A.A. = free of all average 全損賠償

F.P.A. = free from particular average
平安險；單獨海損不賠

G/A = general average 共同海損

M.I. = marine insurance 海上保險

M.I.P. = marine insurance policy
海上保險單

P/A, P.A. = particular average
單獨海損

P&I = protection and indemnity
意外險

T.L.O. = total loss only 僅保全損險

W.A. = with average 單獨海損賠償
險；水漬險

W.P.A. = with particular average
單獨海損賠償

W.R. = war risk 兵險

明信片・卡片

CHAPTER 6

　　許多忙碌的現代人，平時無暇與親友促膝長談、維繫情感，唯有在節日或喜慶時，藉一小小的卡片或明信片來傳達祝福與問候之意。然而您是否有過這樣的煩惱——興致勃勃地想用英文寫些祝福語，可是左思右想，空有滿腔的情意，但卻無法訴諸文字來表達。本章的目的便在幫助讀者解決上述的窘境。我們提供了耶誕卡、賀年卡、母親卡、父親卡、教師卡、情人卡、生日卡、結婚卡，以及明信片的寫作範例。其生動活潑、深情款款的祝福語，除了能增添卡片的風采，也可讓您的真心誠意躍然紙上。

Unit 1 ► 明信片 POST CARD

明信片為長方形的硬紙卡片，由於沒有信封，內容外露，所以稱為明信片。依其特性可分為一般明信片與風景明信片，寫法略有不同。

▶ 一般明信片

正面左上欄寫寄信人姓名、地址(可省略)，右下欄寫收信人姓名、地址，郵票貼於右上角。通信內容寫在背面，不必再重覆Heading、Inside Address，但日期需標上。

POST CARD

Stevie Wu
8, Lane 505
Chung Shan N. Rd., Sec. 5
Taipei, Taiwan

⇧
寄信人姓名、地址

收信人姓名、地址
⇩

Miss Cindy Chen
1050 Benton St.
Apt. #1208
Santa Clara, CA 95050
U.S.A.

▶ 風景明信片

正面是風景或圖片，背面分左右兩欄，左欄寫通信內容，右欄寫收信人姓名、地址，郵票同樣貼在右上角。寄信人地址通常省略，若有必要可寫在通信欄的右上角。

　　明信片空間有限、內容又公開，書寫時應儘量簡略並避免談及機密。結尾謙辭可只寫Sincerely或Yours，全部省略也可以。能縮寫的字就儘量縮寫，以節省空間。

YOKOHAMA Bay Bridge

Tokyo
Sep. 15. 1998

Dear Anna.

We have arrived in Tokyo without any problems. Tokyo is a beautiful and modern city. Here is a postcard of the Yokohama Bay Bridge. The maritime museum at the bottom is splendid. I love the old ships. We are having a great time and hope to see you when we get back.

　　　　　　　　Yours.
　　　　　　　　Joseph

PLACE STAMP HERE

POST CARD

Ms. Anna Wu
4F. 11. Lane 200
Tung Hwa St.
Taipei. Taiwan
R.O.C.

明信片（一）

January 5, 1998

Dear Mom,

It has been great skiing these last few days. There is fresh powder and the weather is perfect. I am really improving and don't worry, I am keeping away from the dangerous slopes. I have met lots of great people, especially one particular girl. I shall introduce her to you when I come home next week.

With love from your son,

1998 年 1 月 5 日

親愛的媽媽：

過去這幾天來滑雪實在是太好玩了。有新下的雪，天氣也正好。我大有進步，您別擔心，我會避開那些險坡的。我遇到許多不錯的人，尤其是一個很特別的女孩。我下禮拜回家後，會介紹她給您認識。

愛子

明信片（二）

July 8, 1998

Dear Susanna,

　　The scenery here is stunning. We swim, sail and fish all day long.　In the evening there is a great band at the pub by the lake shore. We are having a wonderful time.　I hope you are also having a great vacation and are doing well.

　　　　　　　　　　　　Love,

1998年7月8日

親愛的蘇珊娜：

　　這裏的景色美極了！我們整天游泳、出航、釣魚，湖畔有個酒吧，晚上時有個很棒的樂團在這裏表演。我們玩得很盡興，希望妳的假期也過得愉快，事事順利。

　　　　　　　　　　　　上

** have a good〔wonderful〕time 玩得愉快
（＝ *have fun ＝ enjoy oneself* ）

Unit 2 ▶ 卡片 CARD

　　卡片的種類繁多，從最常見的聖誕卡、賀年卡，到母親卡、生日卡、情人卡等，可說琳瑯滿目，應有盡有。市面上販售的卡片，上面已印好祝賀語，只需填上對方的名字，再簽上自己的名字即可。但若能運用巧思，寫出心中的話，將會使收卡人倍感溫馨。

　　歐美的問候卡以聖誕卡為主，由於西風東漸，國內寫聖誕卡的風氣也相當鼎盛。在美國，只要過了感恩節，就可開始寄聖誕卡，賀卡需在耶誕節前寄達，否則即失去意義。由於和新年日期相近，也有人將兩者合併祝賀。需注意的是，給非基督徒的賀詞最好以 *Season's greetings* 或 *Happy holidays* 代替Merry Christmas。

西洋節日一覽表	
情人節《 2 月 14 日》 Valentine's Day	婦女節《 3 月 8 日》 Women's Day
復活節《 3 月 21 日，或該日後 月圓以後的第一個星期天》 Easter Sunday	愚人節《 4 月 1 日》 April Fool's Day
母親節《 5 月第 2 個星期天》 Mother's Day	美國父親節《 6 月 15 日》 Father's Day
感恩節《 11 月第四個星期四》 Thanksgiving（Day）	聖誕節《 12 月 25 日》 Christmas

耶誕卡

To my dear friend Caroline,

I hope you are well and everything is going fine with you. I just want to tell you I am thinking of you and wish you a Merry Christmas and a Happy New Year.

Your friend,

親愛的卡洛琳：

願妳一切安好，事事順利。我只是想告訴妳，我想念妳。祝妳聖誕快樂，新年如意。

USEFUL EXPRESSIONS ··············

* May peace and happiness be with you always. 願和平、快樂常伴你左右。
* Wishing you a white Christmas. 祝你有個白色耶誕節。
* Best wishes on this holiday season. 聖誕佳節最誠摯的祝福。

賀年卡

To my best friend Sam,

I would like to wish you a Happy New Year and hope you have happiness and good fortune in the coming year.

Love,

山姆吾友：

祝你新年快樂！願你在新的一年裡，幸福快樂，好運連連。

USEFUL EXPRESSIONS ·············

* I hope that you will have a prosperous new year. 祝你有個豐收的一年。
* Wishing you the best of luck in the new year. 祝你新年行大運。
* I hope all goes well in the coming year. 祝你在新的一年裏，萬事如意。

母親卡

Dear Mom,

It is only due to your love, care and understanding that we are able to give you this today. Although it cannot possibly adequately express our love, we all wish you the happiest Mother's Day!

Your children,

親愛的媽媽:

完全由於您的關愛與瞭解,我們今天才有能力送您這份禮物。或許它無法適當地表達出我們心中的愛,我們還是祝福您有個最快樂的母親節。

USEFUL EXPRESSIONS ···············

* When I was sick, you always stayed with me. 當我生病時,您總是陪伴著我。
* I may not often say it, but I do love you.
  也許我不常掛在嘴邊,但我真的愛您。

父親卡

Dear Dad,

Here is a card and a gift from far away. Although we are separated by a great distance, my love and respect for you is as strong as ever. Take care and I hope to see you very soon.

Your son,

親愛的爸爸：

獻上我這遠方來的卡片與禮物。雖然我們如今相隔遙遠，我對您的愛和尊敬依然如昔。請多加保重，希望很快就能與您相見。

USEFUL EXPRESSIONS ·············

* You are the best dad in the world. 您是世界上最好的爸爸。

* All my love to the dearest father in the world.
  將我全部的愛，獻給最親愛的爸爸。

* Your experience and guidance have always been appreciated.
  您的經歷和引導，一直讓我衷心感激。

教師卡

Dear Sir,

We all love having you as our teacher.
Although we sometimes misbehave, we hope
you will go on forgiving us.

From all the class of 108

親愛的老師：

我們都喜愛有您當我們的老師。雖然我們
有時候不守規矩，但希望您還是會原諒我們。

108 班全體學生敬上

USEFUL EXPRESSIONS ··············

* This special day is for us to say thank you. 這是讓我們向您說聲謝謝的日子。
* This card is only a small token of our gratefulness.
  這張卡片代表我們的感激之心。
* I promise that I will do better in school. 我保證以後在校一定會表現更好。

情人卡

Dear Michelle,

After such a long time together, I couldn't begin to tell you how much I love you.   You provide me with unending happiness.   You give my life stability and meaning.   On this Valentine's Day I want to tell you of my eternal love and devotion.   I will love you forever.

With love,

親愛的蜜雪兒：

　　經過這麼久的交往，我無法再重頭細說我對你的愛意。妳帶給我無盡的幸福，妳賦予我的生命安定與意義。欣逢情人節，我要對你宣告我永恆的愛意與執著。我愛妳直到永遠。

** stability 〔stə'bɪlətɪ〕 *n.* 安定
　 eternal 〔ɪ'tɜnl̩〕 *adj.* 永恆的

生日卡

Dear Kathy,

　　Here's hoping that your birthday will
be gloriously happy with good friends and
laughter from dawn to dusk.

　　　　　　　　　　　Love,

親愛的凱西：

　　祝福你在摯友及歡笑的環繞下，度過一個多采
多姿的生日。

USEFUL EXPRESSIONS ··············

* Birthday greetings to you and many happy returns of the day.
  祝你福如東海，壽比南山。
* May your birthday and every other day be filled with happiness.
  願你的生日以及每一天，都充滿了快樂。

結婚卡

Dear Jack and Dianne,

On the occasion of your wedding I wish the two of you great happiness, prosperity and a long life together.

Your friend,

親愛的傑克與黛安：

在你們步入結婚禮堂之際，我祝福你倆幸福美滿、白頭到老。

USEFUL EXPRESSIONS ···············

* The two of you make a perfect couple. 你們倆是天造地設的一對。
* Marriage is a life of sharing. 婚姻是分享生活的一切。
* You two are the prince and princess in a fairy tale and may you live happily ever after. 你倆猶如童話中的王子與公主，祝你們從此幸福快樂。

THE STORIES OF CARDS

卡片的起源

問候卡的歷史，可上溯至西元前六世紀的埃及。當時的人們流行在新年時，互贈香水壺作爲賀禮，並在壺上刻著「祈求幸運」等的文字。這種習俗一直流傳至古羅馬時期。

新年時交換問候語的習慣，在基督教時代的歐洲繼續流行。但要到十五世紀時，始出現畫有圖案的卡片，然而當時尚未大量製造。英人 J. C. 賀立茲於西元一八四三年，首先設計了第一張聖誕卡，並用石版印製一千張。之後隨著印刷技術的進步，以及郵政制度的發達，節日互贈卡片的習俗才普及開來。

情人節的由來

西方人流行在二月十四日的「聖華倫泰節」(*St. Valentine's Day*)，互贈卡片及巧克力。對情侶而言，這是愛的表現；對尚未有男友的女孩子，這無疑是向心儀對象表白愛意的大好機會；但若是同事、朋友間，則純粹代表關懷、感謝和友誼之類的涵意。

隨著西風東漸，台灣、以及鄰近的日本、大陸、韓國等地也流行起這股風潮。每逢「聖華倫泰節」，亦即情人節，市面上總是充斥著琳琅滿目的巧克力與情人節禮物，當然，賓館這類場所也是門庭若市，一房難求。

情人節是爲紀念殉教者聖華倫泰(St. Valentine)而定的。關於華

倫泰的故事有不同的版本。據說他在殉教前，曾留下一封淒美的訣別書，給一位在監獄看護他的盲女，上面署名著「寫自你的華倫泰」。人們景仰他忠貞的宗教情操，也爲紀念這段淒美的愛情故事，因此，將他步上斷頭台殉教的那一天定爲情人節。

　　然而在情人節寫卡片的習俗，和華倫泰的殉教並無直接的關聯，倒與早春鳥類的交配期，或是古羅馬的牧羊節(*Lupercalia*)有關。據說在這一天(二月十五日)，男孩子會從大壺裡取出一封情書，交給自己喜歡的女孩子，以求打動伊人的芳心。

投訴・投書

在現今個人主義與民主當道的時代，個人的權益愈來愈受到重視，每個人都有話要說。表達己見的方法很多，有人喜歡訴諸行動、有人動口、有人選擇用文字……每種方法適用的情況不同，所收到的效果也不一樣。在媒體充斥的當今，若能以投訴或投書的方式，將己身的想法傳遞開來，常可獲得不少共鳴。許多公共設施之所以能得到改善，常是群眾以電話、信件砲轟有關當局或是公開在媒體上的結果。為了讓個人的權利不受損害，我們在這章就來談談寫投訴、投書信函的技巧。

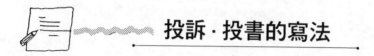

投訴・投書的寫法

投訴信函（*Complaint Letter*）

　　信譽可靠的公司對顧客的來信都極重視，尤其是投訴信函。顧客有所批評即表示產品有缺陷，能藉由投訴信及早發現問題並予以補救改正，將可減少公司的損失。政府機構的角色猶如公司企業，爲求進步，亦應暢開管道，廣納民衆的批評與建言。而人民是國家的主人，對於不當的政策，都有權利申訴。投訴信是鞭策進步的動力，然而部份投訴者只顧怒罵與批評，讓人摸不清其訴求，雖然達到洩恨的目的，仍得不到實質的解決。

　　有效的投訴信應避免激烈的言辭。冷靜、條理地說明問題所在，並提出希望的賠償辦法或解決之道，才能確保自身的權益。產品的使用手册上，多寫有申訴管道，任何方面的問題都可寄到該地址去；對於施政不滿，可透過民意代表來傳達，也可逕向有關單位表態。

報章雜誌（*Newspaper/Magazine*）

　　報章雜誌非常歡迎讀者來函，因爲讀者的意見反映刊物的品質，可作爲改進的指標。報章雜誌多設有讀者意見欄，不但可作溝通的橋樑，一方面也充實版面。然而投書者衆，可刊出的空間有限，如何才能讓自己的意見獲得欣賞？以下是一些建議：

★**簡短扼要**：如上所述，讀者的意見繁多，甚至有重疊的部份，因此編輯在挑選時，多考慮簡短扼要的內容。

★**條理有序**：部份投書天馬行空，毫無條理可言，連編輯閱讀都有困難，何況是一般讀者？好的文章宜在第一句就點出主旨，再把論點有條不紊地闡明清楚。

★**迅速動筆**：有關時事的投稿要儘快動筆，一旦新聞熱度減退，新鮮感不再，被刊登的機率就極微渺。

★**專業知識**：在信中加入專業知識，等於加重說服力，增加刊載的機會，編輯喜歡挑選教授的投書，正是基於此理。

電視·廣播（ *TV / Radio* ）

群眾是媒體推銷的對象，對於觀眾的批評與指教，媒體是歡迎之至。批評節目是媒體最常接到的投書類，書寫時需明確指出節目名稱、播出時段、抗議性質等，如此媒體方能知道如何改進。至於其他疑問，如播映時間、節目的音樂資料等，都可向媒體查詢，得到解答。

近來廣播節目流行聽眾信箱，由主持人在空中讀信，接受點歌。面對雪花般的來信，主持人常會挑選與眾不同的外型或內容來回覆。因此，若希望達到點歌目的，不妨在信封上作些變化，或在內容上添加新意。此外，為方便主持人作業，宜把點播的歌曲、演唱者及播出時間註明清楚。

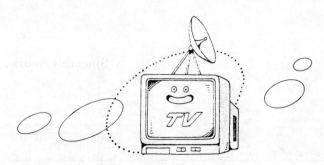

投訴信函

March 5, 1998

Dear Ma'am or Sir,

For years my children have enjoyed your games, which we have found to be of excellent quality. However, I purchased your latest game for my son's birthday. I was told that the game was fully compatible with our machine. After we put the cartridge into the machine, we found that the quality of the graphics and sound was below standard.

As I was told that the product is guaranteed, I would like to enquire as to the cause of the trouble and what steps, if any, I can take to get the game replaced. Any assistance in this matter would be appreciated.

Sincerely yours,

Complaint Letter

1998 年 3 月 5 日

敬啓者：

　　多年來，我的小孩一直很喜歡你們的遊戲卡帶，我們覺得品質優良。然而，我買了你們最新的遊戲卡帶，作爲我兒子的生日禮物。我被告知該卡帶和我們的主機完全符合，但當我們將卡帶插入主機後，卻發現畫面及音效品質低落。

　　既然該產品是附保證書的，我想請教一下毛病出在哪裡，以及我該採取什麼方法，以退換該遊戲卡帶。若能給予協助，不勝感激。

敬上

**　purchase〔ˈpɝtʃəs〕*v*. 購買
　compatible〔kəmˈpætəbḷ〕*adj*. 相容的
　cartridge〔ˈkɑrtrɪdʒ〕*n*. 卡匣

投訴回函

March 10, 1998

Dear Mr. Houston,

We regret to hear that the game you purchased was substandard. Unfortunately, defects in our manufacturing process for our latest game were only discovered after some units had been sold.

We would like to extend our apologies for any trouble this may have caused you and we will of course replace the game, at no extra cost.

Yours sincerely,

Reply to a Complaint Letter

1998 年 3 月 10 日

休斯頓先生：

　　我們很抱歉您購買到劣質的遊戲。很遺憾的，我們直到售出幾套遊戲後，才發現製造過程出了毛病。

　　我們為所引起的困擾，致上歉意，當然，我們也會讓您免費換新。

敬上

＊＊ substandard〔ˏsʌbˈstændəd〕*adj.* 低於標準
defect〔dɪˈfɛkt〕*n.* 缺點
manufacturing〔ˏmænjəˈfæktʃəɪŋ〕*adj.* 製造的

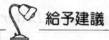

給予建議

April 12, 1998

Dear Sir,

I am a great admirer of your magazine and have been an avid reader for many years. However as the years have gone by, while my appreciation has not faltered, my eyesight has. This is especially a problem when I read my favorite column "About the Town."

I, and a number of my equally elderly friends, find the type far too small to read clearly. Could you please change to a slightly larger type as this would be greatly appreciated by many of your older subscribers.

Yours sincerely,

Giving Advice

1998 年 4 月 12 日

敬啓者：

　　我是貴雜誌的景仰者也是多年的忠實讀者。隨著歲月的流逝，雖然我對貴刊物的喜愛始終不渝，我的視力卻衰退了，尤其當我閱讀最喜歡的專欄「小鎮花絮」，問題更是嚴重。

　　我、以及一些年齡相仿的朋友，都覺得字體太小看不清楚。不知您能否將字體稍稍換大些？相信多數年長的訂閱者都會很感激的。

敬上

** avid〔ˈævɪd〕*adj.* 渴望的
　 falter〔ˈfɔltə〕*v.* 動搖
　 column〔ˈkɑləm〕*n.* 專欄
　 subscriber〔səbˈskraɪbə〕*n.* 訂購者

糾正錯誤

August 15, 1998

Sir,

In your issue of August 12, you referred to Macao as being a Spanish colony. I am afraid I must point out that Macao is not and never has been Spanish. It is presently administered by Portugal, but is recognized by both the Chinese and Portuguese governments as being Chinese territory temporarily under the control of the Portuguese.

I hope that this clears up any misunderstanding you may have had and that this common error will not appear in your otherwise admirable paper again.

Yours sincerely,

Correcting Errors

1998 年 8 月 15 日

敬啟者：

　　在貴報八月十二日的發行中，提到澳門是西班牙的殖民地。我想我恐怕得指出，澳門不是，也從來不曾屬於西班牙。澳門現受葡萄牙管轄，但是中葡兩國政府都承認，它是暫受葡國管理的中國領土。

　　我希望能藉此釐清你們存有的誤解，也希望此一常犯的錯誤，不要再出現在受人讚賞的貴報中。

　　　　　　　　　　　　　　　　　　　　敬上

** *refer to* 提及　　colony〔'kɑlənı〕*n.* 殖民地
　　Macao〔mə'kɑʊ〕*n.* 澳門
　　territory〔'tɛrə,torı〕*n.* 領土
　　temporarily〔'tɛmpə,rɛrəlı〕*adv.* 暫時地
　　Portugal〔'portʃəgļ〕*n.* 葡萄牙
　　Portuguese〔'portʃə,giz〕*n.* 葡萄牙人
　　***clear up* 澄清**

　　　香港為英屬殖民地，1997 年歸還大陸，而澳門現由葡萄牙管理，定 1999 年歸還大陸。

發表意見

August 7, 1995

Sir,

Like many Taipei residents, I have been following the Mass Rapid Transit System saga for many years. I cannot believe after so much time and taxpayers' money we do not yet have a working system or any sign of getting one soon.

I suggest we pay off the contractors immediately and tell them to leave Taiwan. No matter what it costs, it is better to cut our losses now. If Singapore can get a working system below budget and ahead of schedule, I suggest we ask them to come to Taiwan to teach us how it is done.

Yours sincerely,

Your Opinions

1995 年 8 月 7 日

敬啓者：

　　如同許多台北居民一樣，我關心大眾捷運系統的進展已有多年了。我無法相信，在投下這麼多時間與納稅人的金錢之後，我們仍然沒有一個運作體系，或是即將通車的跡象。

　　我建議我們立刻賠償承包商，然後叫他們滾離台灣。不論代價為何，能減低我們的損失總是較好。如果新加坡能在低於預算，且超前進度的情形下，建立一套運輸系統，我建議請新加坡人到台灣來，教教我們人家是如何辦到的。

敬上

**　resident〔'rɛzədənt〕*n.* 居民
　　transit〔'trænsɪt〕*n.* 運輸
　　saga〔'sɑgə〕*n.* 故事
　　taxpayer〔'tæks,peə〕*n.* 納稅人　*pay off* 賠償
　　contractor〔kən'træktə〕*n.* 包商
　　budget〔'bʌdʒɪt〕*n.* 預算

給專欄作家

July 8, 1998

Dear Tabby,

How can I stop my husband from chewing betel nut? When I first met my husband, he had barely begun to chew it. Now he chews it all the time.

I do love my husband, but this unsavory, unhygienic habit disgusts me. What is worse, I have to clean up after him. How can I put an end to this without upsetting my husband?

——Tired of Betel Nut in Tainan

Writing to a Columnist

1998 年 7 月 8 日

親愛的泰比：

　　我該如何讓我的先生停止嚼檳榔？我和他初識時，他幾乎不太嚼，而今他是無時無刻不在嚼檳榔。

　　我真的很愛我先生，但這種氣味難聞又不衛生的習慣，讓我深痛惡絕。更煩人的，我得跟在他後面作清潔工作。我該如何讓他戒掉而又不惹惱他呢？

厭倦檳榔的台南人

**　betel nut〔'bitḷ ˌnʌt〕 *n.* 檳榔
　unsavory〔ʌn'sevərɪ〕 *adj.* 氣味不好的
　unhygienic〔ˌʌnhaɪdʒɪ'ɛnɪk〕 *adj.* 不衛生的
　disgust〔dɪs'gʌst〕 *v.* 使厭惡
　put an end to 終止

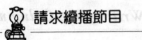

April 24, 1998

Dear Ma'am or Sir,

My family and my friends have enjoyed your program "The Beautiful World of Butterflies" for some time. We find it interesting and educational, so it came as a shock to hear that it will be cancelled.

This show is without doubt the most fascinating program to have appeared on TV. It's educational value far outweighs the fleeting popularity other shows might have. As a public service to the youth of this nation, I ask you to keep this show running.

Sincerely yours,

Supporting a Program

1998 年 4 月 24 日

敬啓者：

　　我的家人及朋友欣賞貴節目「美麗的蝴蝶世界」，已有一段時日。我們覺得這個節目既有趣又富教育性，因此停播的消息讓我們都震驚不已。

　　該節目無疑是現有最吸引人的電視節目。它的教育價值，遠遠超過其他風行一時的節目。就當作是對全國年輕人做一項公衆服務，我請求你們繼續播出該節目。

敬上

** outweigh〔aʊt'we〕*v.* 勝過
　 fleeting〔'flitɪŋ〕*adj.* 短暫的

 詢問節目

June 12, 1998

Dear Ma'am or Sir,

I was very pleased to hear that you will be screening the program "Great Train Journeys of the World". As a train buff you cannot imagine the delight this program is to me.

However I notice that you are only screening fourteen of the fifty available episodes. Do you intend to screen the episodes involving the Peruvian Huaza railway line and the little known Indian Ootermundi steam narrow gauge line? Your answers will be appreciated.

Sincerely yours,

Requesting Information

1998 年 6 月 12 日

敬啓者：

　　很高興聽說貴台要播出「世界火車之旅」。身爲一個火車熱愛者，你們無法想像這個節目將帶給我的快樂。

　　然而，我知道你們只打算播出五十集節目中的十四集。請問你們會播出秘魯化薩鐵路線，以及鮮爲人知的印度兀特穆德狹軌蒸汽鐵路線嗎？期待你們的回音。

敬上

** screen〔skrin〕*v.* 放映
　 buff〔bʌf〕*n.* 熱愛者
　 episode〔'ɛpə,sod〕*n.* 節目中的一集
　 steam〔stim〕*n.* 蒸汽
　 gauge〔gedʒ〕*n.* 軌距

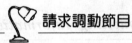 請求調動節目

January 7, 1998

Dear Ma'am or Sir,

I have noticed that your program "Advanced Mahjongg" has been put on at 10:30 at night. This is my grandmother's favorite program but unfortunately she cannot watch this program at this time, due to her charity work.

Would it be possible to move the screening of this program to 11:30 at night when my grandmother will be at home and eagerly awaiting this excellent program?

Yours sincerely,

Broadcast Time

1998 年 1 月 7 日

敬啓者：

　　貴台的節目「進階麻將」，一向在晚間十點半播出。
這是我祖母最喜歡的節目，但她因爲慈善工作的關係，
無法在這時段收看。

　　不知能否請您將播出時間，改至晚間十一點半？這
時我祖母便可在家，滿心期待這精彩的節目。

敬上

** mahjongg〔mɑˈdʒɑn〕 *n.* 麻將（亦作 mahjong）
　charity〔ˈtʃærətɪ〕 *n.* 慈善

批評節目

October 15, 1998

Dear Ma'am or Sir,

On October 9, your station broadcast "Comedy Hour from the Apollo Theater in New York". This American show was entertaining, but there were parts of it I found disturbing.

The crude language and suggestive tone of many of the comedians was in poor taste and not suited for family viewing. Given this, may I ask why it was on at such an early hour when children would be watching? If you wish to continue to attract viewers like myself, I suggest prudence in your evening programming.

Yours sincerely,

Criticizing Programs

1998 年 10 月 15 日

敬啓者：

　　在十月九日，貴台播出「紐約阿波羅劇團喜劇」。這個美國節目具娛樂性，但是其中有些部份令我感到不舒服。

　　劇中多位喜劇演員粗俗的語言、暗示性的口吻，實在沒品味，也不適合全家觀賞。有鑑於此，我不禁要請問一下，該節目爲何在這麼早的時段就播出，讓兒童有機會看到？如果你們想繼續吸引我這樣的觀衆，我建議你們謹愼規劃晚間節目。

敬上

** broadcast〔'brɔd,kæst〕 *v.* 播放
crude〔krud〕 *adj.* 粗糙的
suggestive〔sə'dʒɛstɪv〕 *adj.* 暗示的
prudence〔'prudns〕 *n.* 謹愼

December 3, 1998

Dear Ma'am or Sir,

I am the mother of two children aged nine and seven. After they have done their homework, I allow them to watch two hours of TV in the evening. This enables them to relax before bedtime.

Last night you screened the new traffic safety commercial. While I recognize the need to educate the public about this, showing graphic pictures of accident victims is not the right way. All it does is cause nightmares for my children. Would you please reduce the amount of blood and gore you show or move these ads to a later time?

Yours sincerely,

Criticizing Commercials

1998 年 12 月 3 日

敬啓者：

　　我是兩個九歲和七歲孩子的母親。在他們做完功課後，我允許他們晚上看兩小時的電視，讓他們在睡覺前輕鬆一下。

　　昨晚貴台播放新的交通安全廣告。我能體認教育大眾的需要，然而，播出事故受害者活生生血淋淋的照片，並不是明智的辦法，它只會令我的孩子作惡夢。能否請您減少播出流血的場面，或是把這些廣告移到晚一點的時段？

敬上

**　bedtime〔'bɛd,taɪm〕*n.* 就寢時間
　　commercial〔kə'mɝʃəl〕*n.* 商業廣告
　　graphic〔'græfɪk〕*adj.* 生動的
　　victim〔'vɪktɪm〕*n.* 受害者
　　nightmare〔'naɪt,mɛr〕*n.* 惡夢
　　gore〔gor〕*n.* 流血

點播歌曲

Dear Ron,

Now I am doing my National Military Service in the South of Taiwan. Every day I am very busy so I can neither write to my girlfriend as often as I would like nor express my true feelings to her very well.

In order to let her know how I feel, could you please play "The Greatest Love of All" by Whitney Houston, which expresses my true feelings for her. Thank you.

Lonely in Tainan,
Charles Lin

Requesting Songs

親愛的朗恩：

　　我現在南台灣服役。我每日忙碌，無法時常寫信給
女友，也不知該如何表達我的真情。

　　為了讓她知道我的感受，請你播放惠妮・休斯頓的
「至高的愛」，代我向她表達我的真情。謝謝。

台南的寂寞人

查爾斯・林

** military〔ˈmɪləˌtɛrɪ〕*adj.* 軍事的

INFORMATION · · · · · · · · · · · · · · · ·

　　ICRT（International Community Radio Taipei）的前身
是**AFNT**（American Forces Network Taiwan）美軍電台。自
前美國總統卡特宣布與台灣斷交後，駐台美軍撤走已成定局，
AFNT自然也沒有存在的必要。但一些非軍方的外籍人士深知，
如果這個英語電台就此消失，將對他們的生活造成偌大的不便，
於是營救活動於焉展開。經過多方努力與新聞局的許可，「台北
國際社區電台」在一九七九年四月十六日零時整，正式誕生。
ICRT的現址是台北市陽明山中庸二路八號之一。

 **大衆傳播媒體資料**

The China News 英文中國日報
    Add: 10F, 109-1, Tung Hsing St., Taipei
        台北市東興街 109 之 1 號 10 樓
    Tel: (02)768-6002   Fax: (02)768-6773, 768-6908

The China Post 英文中國日報
    Add: 8 Fushun St., Taiepi
        台北市撫順街 8 號
    Tel: (02)596-9971   Fax: (02)595-7962

The Free China Journal 英文自由中國紀事報
    Add: 2 Tientsin St., Taipei
        台北市天津街 2 號
    Tel: (02)397-0180   Fax: (02)356-8233

Let's Talk in English 大家說英語 / **Studio Classroom** 空中英語教室
    Add: 10, Lane 62, Tachih St., Taipei
        台北市大直街 62 巷 10 號
    Tel: (02)502-9144   Fax: (02)501-1009

Ivy League Analytical English 常春藤解析英語
    Add: 2F, 33 Chunghsiao W. Rd., Sec. 1, Taipei
        台北市忠孝西路一段 33 號 2 樓
    Tel: (02)331-7600   Fax: (02)381-0918

Reader's Digest 讀者文摘
    Add: 2 & 3 Fls, 2 Minsheng E. Rd., Sec. 5, Taipei
        台北市民生東路五段 2 號 2/3 樓
    Tel: (02)746-1500   Fax: (02)762-8187

International Community Radio Taipei (ICRT) 台北國際社區電台
    Add: 8-1 Chungyung 2nd Rd., Shantzehou, Yangmingshan, Taipei
        台北市陽明山山仔后中庸二路 8 號之 1
    Tel: (02)861-2280   Fax: (02)861-3863

通知・啓事・廣告

8

您是否曾注意到，在報章雜誌的各個角落裡，甚至整個版面上，都有著大大小小、各式各樣的廣告、通知或啓事呢？通知、啓事、廣告都屬於公告性的文體，它可以是針對特定的人所發出的，如警告逃妻；也可以是不分對象的宣傳，如商品廣告。這類文體旨在吸引他人的注意，因此醒目的標頭是他們共有的特點。至於書寫的風格，則因人、因事而異，如訃聞屬嚴肅性質，多採用公式化的寫法，而商品廣告因要引起消費者的購買慾，則會選擇新穎、聳動的語彙。在這一章，我們就來看看要如何寫這類的應用文體。

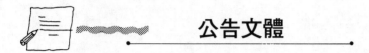

公告文體

通知 (*Announcement*)

通知可採用信函方式，寄給有關人士，也可利用媒體公開昭告。通知信函的寫法同一般社交信函；公開通知（Public Announcement）則為簡略的事實陳述，以**第三人稱**書寫，沒有稱謂。常見的通知類有婚訊、死訊、嬰兒誕生等。

啟事 (*Notice*)

啟事屬於公告性的文體，個人或團體若有事情要向大眾公開說明，可將內容簡單扼要寫成啟事，張貼在**公共場所**。若事情重要，需要廣為人知，可**刊登在報上**。啟事的種類繁多，生活中常用的有遺失啟事、尋人啟事、招領啟事、遷移啟事、徵婚啟事等。

廣告 (*Advertisement*)

廣告主要刊登在報章雜誌上，或以海報的方式，張貼於公共場所。廣告的目的在推銷與介紹，語言的使用應以**簡單、明瞭、醒目**為原則，才能吸引大眾的注意力。好的廣告詞讓人琅琅上口，如某廣告的「有點…又不會太…」已融入群眾的生活中，當人們在套用這句流行語時，自然會聯想到該產品。

上述的例子是商品廣告，在租屋、售屋等小型分類廣告上，也是依此原則書寫。房屋的結構固然要詳細列出，但可採用感性的寫法來打動人心。

◢ **訂婚通知** ◣

Howard-Chen, Mr. and Mrs. J.S. Howard of
Yangmingshan, Taipei, would like to an-
nounce the engagement of their eldest son
D.P. Howard to Ms. Mary Chen, youngest
daughter of Mr. and Mrs. C.K. Chen of
Hsintien, Taipei County.

霍華與陳訂婚啓事──台北陽明山 J.S.霍華夫婦，
宣布長子D.P.霍華，與台北縣新店C.K. 陳夫婦
的幼女陳瑪麗訂婚。

◢ **結婚通知** ◣

Mr. and Mrs. C.J. James are pleased to announce the marriage of their only daughter
Jennifer to Mr. Peter Lin on Thursday, the
eighth of November at the Church of the
Blessed Trinity, Shihlin, Taipei, Taiwan.

C.J.詹姆士夫婦宣布，他們的獨生女珍妮佛和林
彼得先生於11月8日星期四，在台灣台北士林三聖
堂完婚。

---- ✍✎✐ 誕生通知 ✑✒✍ ----

Mr. and Mrs. Sean K.C. Ma of 12 Hoping East Road, announce the birth of a daughter Jane Ma in Taiwan University Hospital on Friday, January 16th.

和平東路12號的史恩K.C. 馬先生夫婦，特此宣告親友，愛女馬珍於一月十六日星期五誕生於台大醫院。

---- ✍✎✐ 訃聞 ✑✒✍ ----

Thomas Lin passed away at Chunghsiao Hospital on the 22nd of September. His funeral will be at Liuchangli Municipal Cemetery, Taipei, on September 30 at 2:00 p.m. Cortege will start from Saint John's Church at 12:30 p.m.

湯瑪斯・林九月二十二日逝於忠孝醫院，九月三十日下午二時將下葬於台北市六張犁公墓。送喪行列中午十二時三十分由聖約翰教堂開始。

    ** municipal〔mju'nɪsəpḷ〕*adj*. 市的
        cortege〔kɔr'teʒ〕*n*. 行列

LOST

I lost a copy of the Far East Chinese English Dictionary while studying in the Library Reading Room. If anyone finds it, will they please hand it in to the Chinese Department Office or ring me at (05)278-3279.

John Lin

遺　失　啓　事

本人於圖書館閱覽室，遺失了一本遠東漢英字典。若有人尋獲，煩請送至中文系辦公室，或電(05)278-3279與我聯絡。

林約翰

LOST CHILD

My daughter, Chen Mei-ling, disappeared on the afternoon of March 14th when returning from school. She is seven years old, 1.20 meters with an oval face, big eyes, and long hair.

Whoever finds her, has any knowledge of her whereabouts or has any information that might lead to her discovery is requested to contact local police or her family at 235 Beiping Road, (02)363-2766.

Chen Wen-long

尋　人　啓　事

　　小女陳美玲於三月十四日下午，自學校返家途中失蹤。她現年七歲，身高120公分，瓜子臉、大眼睛、蓄長髮。

　　若有任何人找到她，或有她的下落，以及任何能尋獲她的消息，請聯絡當地警方或是她的家人。地址是北平路235號，電話（02）363-2766。

陳文龍

**　oval〔'ovḷ〕*adj.* 橢圓形的

whereabouts〔'hwɛr,baʊts〕*n.* 下落

　　（可作單數或複數用）

request〔rɪ'kwɛst〕*v.* 請求

FOUND

Yesterday a purse was found in our class-room containing a small sum of money, a few tickets and some keys. Anyone who has lost a purse recently can come to Rm 102 and describe the lost purse.

George Wu

失 物 招 領

本班教室內昨拾獲一皮夾，內有少數現金、車票及鑰匙。若有人最近遺失皮夾，請至102教室認領。

吳喬治

RELOCATION

Due to the rapid expansion of our business we have found it necessary to move to larger premises. Starting from October 11th we shall be at 102 Tunghwa Street. We apologize for any inconvenience we may have caused.

Management
Elephant Restaurant

遷 移 啓 事

本店因業務擴展迅速，場地不敷使用必須搬遷，自十月十一日起，移至通化街102號。諸多不便，敬請原諒。

大象餐廳經理

** expansion〔ɪkˈspænʃən〕*n.* 擴張
　 premises〔ˈprɛmɪsɪz〕*n. pl.* 房屋

SEEKING A SPOUSE

David, 30, graduate of UCLA, presently Systems Manager for First National Bank, non-smoker, non-drinker, interested in sports and outdoor activities, has house with pool, seeks an honest, sincere, warm female for long-term relationship. Photo preferable. All replies will be answered. If interested please contact (03)278-4345 or Post Office Box 89.

徵 婚 啓 事

大衞，現年三十，加州大學洛杉磯分校畢業，現任第一國際銀行系統部經理。無煙酒習慣，嗜好運動與戶外活動，有自宅，內有游泳池。欲徵篤實、眞誠、親切的女性爲伴侶。附照片爲佳，所有來信均予受理。意者請電（03)278-4345 或寫信至郵政信箱89號。

** ***UCLA*** 是 University of California at Los Angeles
（加州大學洛杉磯分校）的縮寫
preferable〔'prɛf(ə)rəbḷ〕 *adj*. 較佳的

SEEKING A SPOUSE

Attractive, long hair, creative, philosophical, 26 y.o. female, primary school teacher who is financially secure, enjoys music, dancing, movies, theater, painting and books, would like to meet intelligent, sincere, attractive male for a possible permanent relationship. Ideally 26-30 y.o. Please send photo. Write to 147 Nanyang Street, Taipei.

徵 婚 啓 事

　　長髮動人、富創意、達觀女性。芳齡26 , 任教小學 , 經濟穩定。愛好音樂、舞蹈、電影、戲劇、繪畫、閱讀。欲徵求聰明、誠懇的英俊男士為終生伴侶。理想年齡26～30歲 , 請附照片 , 來函請寄台北市南陽街147號。

**　philosophical〔͵fɪlə'sɑfɪkl̩〕*adj.* 達觀的
　　primary school 小學
　　secure〔sɪ'kjʊr〕*adj.* 穩固的
　　permanent〔'pɝmənənt〕*adj.* 永久的

HELP WANTED

Opening for Executive Assistant. Must type at least 60 wpm with shorthand of 80 wpm or above. Job involves working with busy marketing executive. Good working conditions, competitive starting salary, benefits. For interview call (02)808-4458.

求 才 廣 告

誠徵行政助理，每分鐘須能打60字以上，速記80字以上，協助市場部主管處理繁忙事務。工作環境佳、起薪優渥、福利好。請電(02)808-4458安排面談。

** opening〔'op(ə)nɪŋ〕*n.* 職位空缺
executive〔ɪg'zɛkjʊtɪv〕*adj.*行政的　*n.*主管人員
wpm 是 word per minute 的縮寫
shorthand〔'ʃɔrt,hænd〕*n.* 速記

ROOM FOR RENT

Room available for two in a private home.
Extensively furnished.   Near public trans-
port — only 10 minutes from center of town.
Rent $5,000 a month utilities not included.
Call 359-8798.

雅 房 出 租

私人住宅雙人房出租。傢俱齊全，近大衆交通設
備——離市中心僅需十分鐘。月租五仟，不含水
電，請電洽359-8798。

** furnish 〔ˈfɜnɪʃ〕 *v*. 陳設
utility 〔juˈtɪlətɪ〕 *n*. 公共設施 (自來水、電氣等)

HOUSE FOR SALE

Handsome five bedroom house for sale.
Large family room. Fireplaces. Large
garden bordering lake. Located on secluded
lane. Ideal for family seeking privacy.
$8,500,000.

吉 屋 出 售

五房美觀住宅出售。客廳寬敞，有壁爐、湖
濱花園。座落清幽巷道，適合尋找隱蔽空間
的家庭。總價 850 萬元。

** fireplace 〔'faɪr,ples〕 *n.* 壁爐
　　secluded 〔sɪ'kludɪd〕 *adj.* 隔絕的
　　privacy 〔'praɪvəsɪ〕 *n.* 隱蔽

CAR FOR SALE

1989 TOYOTA CAMRY, 4 dr Sedan, Power steering and brakes. 10,000 miles. Original owner. Air cond. Call (02)987-6543.

轎 車 出 售

八九年豐田冠美麗，四門轎車，動力方向盤及刹車系統。已跑一萬英哩，第一位車主。備空調。意者請電(02)987-6543。

** sedan 〔sɪˈdæn〕 *n.* 轎車
steering 〔ˈstɪrɪŋ〕 *n.* 方向盤
brake 〔brek〕 *n.* 煞車

商品/服務廣告

Ever Quick Plumbing

Fast Plumbing Service
No call out fee
Ring (02)313-3849
We guarantee our results

馬上通水管公司

服務迅速
免車馬費
請電(02)313-3849
服務品質保證

** plumbing〔ˈplʌmɪŋ〕*n.* 水管工程

電報・傳真

　　Facsimile(傳真)簡稱 Fax ，是目前
最時興與便利的通訊工具。它能突破時
空的障礙,將訊息以最快的速度傳到目
的地。從前由於造價昂貴的關係,使得
傳真機雖有強大的功能,但在經濟因素
的考量下,卻不若電傳(Telex)來得普
及。而今在量產下,其價格節節下降,
幾乎每家公司都擁有傳真設備,甚至也
有人將之用來傳送股市行情呢!有鑑
於傳真的便利與經濟(其計費比照電話
費),本書特闢此章節,將傳真英文的
寫作要領介紹給讀者。當然我們也會在
此順便談談和傳真一樣快捷的電報。

Unit 1 ► 電報 TELEGRAM

　　遇有緊急事件需通知他人，電報無疑是最迅速、最簡便的方法。國際電報可拍發到世界各地，甚至航行中的船隻與空中的飛機，可謂**無遠弗屆**。電報費以字數計算，因此內容應力求**簡潔**，以節省花費，以下是拍發電報的注意事項：

◆為使內容醒目，每個字的開頭可用**大寫**或全用大寫。標點符號一般都不使用，為區分上下句義，可用 STOP 表示句號。

◆為節省費用，可省略冠詞、助動詞、介系詞等虛詞，**保留實詞**部份。省略第一、第二人稱的主詞亦無妨。

◆電報中常用現在分詞表未來的計畫。發報人所做的事也以現在分詞表示，而要求收報人所做的事則用祈使句，如：

COMING HOME SOON ＝ I shall come home soon.
COME HOME SOON ＝ Please come home soon.

◆短的詞組可**合併為一字**，如 as soon as 變成 ASSOONAS，New York 併為 NEWYORK。

祝賀生日

MANY HAPPY RETURNS ON YOUR BIRTHDAY
WISHING BEST LUCK AND GOOD HEALTH

祝你生日快樂，長壽健康。

祝賀結婚

HAPPY ABOUT YOUR MARRIAGE WISHING YOU
BOTH A LONG HAPPY LIFE TOGETHER

喜聞婚訊，祝你倆永遠幸福快樂。

祝賀陞遷

CONGRATULATIONS ON RECENT PROMOTION
TO SYSTEMS OPERATOR WISHING FURTHER
SUCCESS

恭喜晉升系統主管，祝步步高升。

祝賀金榜題名

CONGRATULATIONS ON PHD EXAM RESULT

恭喜通過博士考試。

生產通知

BOY BORN LAST NIGHT MOTHER AND
BABY DOING WELL

男孩昨晚誕生，母子平安。

住院通知

MOTHER ILL IN HOSPITAL COME HOME

母病住院，請回家。

報平安

GRANDMOTHER ARRIVED SAFELY YESTERDAY
STOP LETTER TO FOLLOW

祖母昨安抵家，信另寄。

緊急事故

SOMETHING WRONG COME SOON MUCH
TO DISCUSS

出事速回，有事商討。

• 意外事故 •

CAR ACCIDENT DAVID INJURED BETTER NOW

大衛車禍受傷，好多了。

• 弔唁 •

DEEPEST CONDOLENCES ON DEATH OF YOUR
FATHER PRAYING FOR YOU

為令尊逝世致上深切哀悼，為你們禱告。

• 謝絕邀請 •

THANKS FOR KIND INVITATION SORRY
CANNOT COME

謝謝邀請，抱歉無法前去。

命名 HOPE 的故事

　　曾經有個紐約商人，駕駛自用飛機前往阿拉斯加洽談商務，他的太太當時正身懷六甲。這名商人在前往阿拉斯加途中，因爲遇到大雪被迫降機，而發生了一點小事故。此時他太太來了一封電報問道：「你還好嗎？我已經生了一個很可愛的男孩。要如何命名呢？」

　　這個商人馬上回了這樣的電報：

"CANNOT THINK OF GOOD NAME BUT HOPE EVERYTHING OK"

　　不久之後這個商人回到了家，抱著可愛的男嬰問道：「叫什麼名字？」，太太回答：「叫 Hope」，商人滿臉疑惑地說：「爲何取這樣的名字？」，太太趕忙回答：「你電報上不是這麼說的嗎？」

　　這個商人後來才發現個中原委：他的原意是 *"I cannot think of a good name, but I hope everything is OK (there)."*（我想不出適當的名字，但是希望你那裡一切安好。），但他的太太卻誤解成 *"I cannot think of a good name but(= except) Hope. Everything is OK (here)."*（除了 Hope 之外，我想不出適當的名字，這裡一切安好。）

　　可見句點 STOP 的使用應詳加斟酌。

Unit 2 ▶ 傳眞 FAX

FAX 的使用要領

　　傳眞的發明與引進是商業界的一大福音。從前爲了聯絡地球彼端的客戶，職員常得深夜留在辦公室裏。但使用傳眞機後，克服了時差問題，資料、文件可直接先傳送過去，無形中減少了時間與人力的浪費。傳眞方便易操作，但因人爲的疏失，不免降低其效率。以下是一些使用傳眞的要訣：

- ♥ 發信與收信雙方都需負擔紙的費用，所以應避免傳垃圾文件。傳大量文件時，應先通知對方準備足量的紙張。

- ◆ 有部份人利用傳眞發廣告，因此，對收到的文件要謹愼過濾，小心勿將重要文件當成廣告而丟棄。

- ♠ 傳眞前先以電話通知對方，說明何時傳出、所需花費的時間。

- ♣ 傳眞前檢查文件是否齊全。

FAX 英文文法

　　傳眞講究速率與時效，因此可省略客套語，直接切入主題，不必拘泥書信的格式。在文字上，只要意思通達不致誤解，可將 I 、 we 等主詞省略。助動詞類如 have 、 could 、 would 在不拘泥差異的情形下，也可不寫。例如：

> We will not be able to...→ Unable to...
> We have received...→ Received

　　省略的方法雖有其優點，但不可任意刪減，應以清楚、明瞭為優先考量。又如弔唁、祝賀類等較正式的信函，為求禮貌起見，在用語或格式上（稱謂、結尾謙辭），則不可省略。

　　簡寫也是節省時間的好辦法，如 as soon as possible 便可用 **ASAP** 代替，但是也不宜濫用，如 Pls.是電傳(Telex)上 please 的略語，但並不廣為人知。此外，日期也要詳細書寫，除非在傳真開頭有註明發信的日期，否則應避免單獨使用 tomorrow、 next Monday 之類的詞彙。因為接收的一方很可能在日後才看到該文件，而傳真上的 tomorrow、 next Monday 也早過期了。

FAX 的格式

　　理想的傳真格式至少應包含下列各項目：

(1) 發信人所屬的單位　　　　(7) 收信人所屬的單位

(2) 發信人的姓名　　　　　　(8) 收信人的姓名

(3) 發信人的地址　　　　　　(9) 收信人的傳真號碼

(4) 發信人的電話號碼　　　　(10) 收信人的電話號碼

(5) 發信人的傳真號碼　　　　(11) 文件的張數

(6) 發信的日期　　　　　　　(12) 通訊欄

　　以上所列的各項可依公司、所屬單位、或個人業務的性質來作適度的變化與刪減，例如將(9)、(10)項省略並無影響。以下是一份傳真的格式範例供作讀者參考：

☑Evergreen Publishing Company [1]

65, Lane 63, Tunhua South Rd., Sec.2, Taipei, Taiwan [2]
Tel:886-2-678-2345 [3]　Fax: 886-2-687-9876 [4]

TO: _____ [5]　**TEL:** _____ [6]

COMPANY: _____ [7]　**FAX :** _____ [8]

FROM: _____ [9]　**DATE:** _____ [10]

NUMBER OF PAGES INCLUDING THIS ONE: _____ [11]

MESSAGE: [12]

---

1) 發信人所屬的單位	2) 發信人的地址	3) 發信人的電話號碼
4) 發信人的傳眞號碼	5) 收信人的姓名	6) 收信人的電話號碼
7) 收信人所屬的單位	8) 收信人的傳眞號碼	9) 發信人的姓名
10) 發信的日期	11) 文件的張數	12) 通訊欄

謝絕報價

10/24/98
Date

TO: 886-2-494-3813 　　**ATTN**: Bill Washington
FROM: Joey Johnson
NO. OF PAGES INCLUDING THIS ONE: 1

MESSAGE:

Thank you for your prompt message of October 10. Sorry that there has been a delay in replying due to my business in Singapore.

Unfortunately your quotation was above our maximum acceptable price.

Should the opportunity arise, I will contact you again about further business deals.

Declining an Offer

日期：**98** 年 **10** 月 **24** 日

傳給：886-2-494-3813　　　收件人：比爾・華盛頓

發自：喬伊・強森

頁碼：**1**

訊息：

感謝您 10 月 10 日隨即傳來訊息，抱歉由於赴新加坡洽公，所以回覆晚了。

很遺憾，您的報價超過我們所能接受的最高價格。

倘若有機會，我會再與您進一步洽談生意。

Learning Publishing Co., Ltd.

4F, 11, Lane 200, Tunghwa St.,
Taipei, Taiwan
Fax: (02) 707-9095

TO : Mr. Grant　　　**FAX :** 82-2-532-0867

FROM : Stevie Wu　　**DATE :** Feb. 20, 1998

Will be in Yokohama until next Friday. If you have time, I would like to ask you to lunch on Wednesday, March 5. If arrangements can be made, Mr. Brown and Mr. Tanaka will also be there. Please ask if there is any problem and I will get in touch with the details later. Looking forward to seeing you again.

Luncheon

學習出版有限公司

中華民國台灣台北市通化街 200 巷 11 號 4F

傳眞：886‐2‐707‐9095

傳給：格蘭特先生　　　傳眞：　82‐2‐532‐0867

發自：史蒂夫‧吳　　　日期：1998 年 2 月 20 日

會在橫濱待到下星期五。如果你有空，我想請你 3 月 5 日星期三一道午餐。如果約得到，布朗先生和田中先生也會去。請看看有沒有問題，我會再聯絡討論細節。期盼與您再相見。

 **訂購機票**

DATE: September 5, 1998

TO: Japan Asia Airways   **FAX:**（02）777-2993

FROM: Emmy Barton   **FAX:**（02）707-3849

I want to book a round-trip ticket on Japan Asia Airways from Taipei to Tokyo for the 19th of September. I would like to return on the 5th of October. I would like a business class, non-smoking seat. I am a vegetarian, so I would require special meals. The ticket will be charged to my company account. Please fax me with my final itinerary and flight confirmations.

** vegetarian〔͵vɛdʒəˈtɛrɪən〕*n*. 素食者
itinerary〔aɪˈtɪnəͺrɛrɪ, ɪ-〕*n*. 行程
confirmation〔͵kɑnfəˈmeʃən〕*n*. 確定

Booking Airline Seats

日期：1998 年 9 月 5 日

發給：亞細亞航空公司　　　傳眞：(02)777-2993

發自：艾咪・巴頓　　　　　傳眞：(02)707-3849

我想訂購九月十九日，台北至東京的亞細亞航空公司來回機票。我十月五日要返回。我想訂商務艙的非吸煙區。我是素食者，所以需要特別的餐點。機票的錢將記入我公司的帳戶。行程、班機確定後請傳眞給我。

USEFUL EXPRESSIONS ················

* Can I use my EVA Airlines voucher to pay for the ticket？我能使用長榮航空的優待券來支付機票費用嗎？

* Can you mail my ticket to me via express mail？
  (Can you express my ticket？)
  你能以快遞將票寄給我嗎？

* When do I need to reconfirm my return flight？
  我何時需要再確認回程的機位？

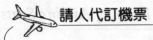 請人代訂機票

DATE：February 1, 1998
TO：Mary Brown
FROM：Sara Li　　　　**FAX**：886-2-395-2086

I am planning to travel to Mexico City on February 14 and stay there for six days. Please book a business class, round-trip ticket leaving Seoul, Korea on the 14th on United Airlines. The Bank of Taiwan is instructed to pay for the ticket and your fee. Submit the account directly to them. Please fax the itinerary ASAP. Thanks for your help.

** instruct〔ɪn'strʌkt〕v. 指示
　　fee〔fi〕n. 報酬
　　submit〔səb'mɪt〕v. 提出
　　ASAP = *as soon as possible*

Booking Seats

日期：1998 年 2 月 1 日
傳給：瑪麗・布朗
發自：莎拉・李　　　傳眞：886- 2- 395- 2086

我計畫二月十四日至墨西哥市旅行六天，請幫我預訂
十四日，從韓國漢城起飛的聯合航空來回商務艙機票。
台灣銀行已收到指示支付機票費用及你的酬勞，請直
接向他們提出帳單。請儘快將行程傳眞給我，謝謝你
的協助。

USEFUL EXPRESSIONS ··············

* (We) require four business class tickets to Anchorage and will reimburse you for the fare and booking fee.
我們需要四張往安克利治的商務艙機票，酬勞與機票的錢將
會付還給你。

* Thank you for your help in reserving a flight for our sales representative.
感謝你爲我方的業務代表預訂機票。

詢問飯店房價

FAX MESSAGE

TO: Downtown Plaza Hotel　　**FAX**: 886-2-707-9035
FROM: Victor Perez　　**TEL**: 886-2-704-5535

I am planning to travel to Los Angeles on the 17th of October and would like a room for five days. Please provide the rates for a single deluxe room. I would also like information on your shuttle services as well as your business meeting facilities. Please fax the information to my office at the number above. Thank you in advance for your services.

＊＊ deluxe〔dɪˈluks, -ʌks〕*adj*. 豪華的
　　shuttle〔ˈʃʌtl̩〕*n*. 往返行駛的車
　　facilities〔fəˈsɪlətɪz〕*n.pl*. 設施
　　in advance 預先

Asking Hotel Room Rates

傳 眞 訊 息

發給：廣場大飯店　　　傳眞：886-2-707-9035

發自：維多·培瑞茲　　　電話：886-2-704-5535

我計畫十月十七日前往洛杉磯，因此想訂五天的房間。請提供我豪華單人房的價格。另外，我也需要貴飯店的接送服務與商務會議設施的資料。請照上面的號碼，將資料傳眞至我的辦公室。在這兒先謝謝您的服務。

USEFUL EXPRESSIONS ·················

* How much does your deluxe suite run per night ?
  貴飯店的豪華套房一晚要多少錢？

* What are your rates for the off-season ? (What are off-season rates ?) 貴飯店的淡季價格如何？

* Do you give discount(s) for tour groups ?
  你們提供折扣給旅行團嗎？

預訂房間

TO: Miami Raddison Hotel

FROM: Fran Wang   **FAX**: 886-2-993-8826

                        TEL: 886-2-913-8215

I would like to book four deluxe single rooms, preferably connected, for the nights of the 12th through the 15th of March. We would like the rooms to be non-smoking, if possible. The rooms will be charged to our company's Master Card. Please call or fax with the confirmation of our reservations.

** preferably 〔'prɛf(ə)rəblɪ〕 *adv*. 最好
   reservation 〔,rɛzə'veʃən〕 *n*. 預約

Making a Reservation

傳給：邁阿密瑞迪森飯店

傳自：法蘭·王　　　傳眞：886-2-993-8826
　　　　　　　　　電話：886-2-913-8215

我想訂三月十二日至十五日幾晚的豪華單人房四間，最好能連房。可能的話，我們想要禁煙的房間。房錢將以本公司的萬事達卡來支付。預約確定後，請打電話或傳眞給我。

USEFUL EXPRESSIONS ·················

* (I) want to make a reservation for a room for tomorrow night. 我要預訂一間明晚的房間。

* (We) would like a room with (a) good view of the harbor. 我們想要一間能眺望港口的房間。

* Does your hotel provide a shuttle to your hotel from the airport? 貴飯店提供機場到飯店的接送服務嗎？

請人代訂房間

Would like to ask you to reserve two rooms
at the Hyatt for our foreign representatives.
Will be arriving the afternoon of the 20th
and will stay for eleven days. Would like
two adjoining single rooms, if possible.
Please notify us when the reservation is
confirmed. Appreciate your help.

想請你為我們的國外代表在凱悅預訂兩間房間。他
們將在二十日下午抵達並停留十一天。可以的話，
要兩間毗鄰的單人房。預約確定後，請通知我們。
感謝您的幫忙。

** representative〔͵rɛprɪ'zɛntətɪv〕*n.* 代表
adjoining〔ə'dʒɔɪnɪŋ〕*adj.* 相鄰的
notify〔'notə͵faɪ〕*v.* 通知

詢問旅遊資料

I am interested in traveling to Hong Kong. I would appreciate any information you could send me. I would particularly like to know round-trip air fare rates from New York City. I plan to depart on the 15th of June and stay for nine days. Please fax me your information ASAP. Thank you.

我有興趣到香港旅遊，若蒙寄上任何資料將至爲感激。我尤其想知道從紐約的來回機票價格。我計畫六月十五日出發並停留九天。請儘快將貴社的資料傳眞給我。謝謝！

** fare〔fɛr〕*n.* 費用　　rate〔ret〕*n.* 價格
depart〔dɪˈpɑrt〕*v.* 出發

INTERNATIONAL DIRECT DIALING
國際電話直撥國碼表

國　　　　　家	國　碼	城　　　　　　　市	城市碼
Argentina 阿根廷	54	Buenos Aires 布宜諾斯艾利斯	1
Australia 澳大利亞	61	Melbourne 墨爾本	3
		Sydney 雪梨	2
Austria 奧地利	43	Vienna 維也納	1
Bangladesh 孟加拉	880		
Belgium 比利時	32	Brussels 布魯賽爾	2
Belize 貝里斯	501		
Bolivia 玻利維亞	591		
Brazil 巴西	55	Rio de Janeiro 里約	21
		Sao Paulo 聖保羅	11
Canada 加拿大	1	Montreal 蒙特婁	514
		Quebec 魁北克	418
		Toronto 多倫多	416
		Vancouver 溫哥華	604
Chile 智利	56	Santiago 聖地牙哥	2
Colombia 哥倫比亞	57	Bogota 波哥大	1
Costa Rica 哥斯大黎加	506		
Czechoslovakia 捷克	42	Prague 布拉格	2
Denmark 丹麥	45		
Dominican Rep. 多明尼加	1	Santiago 聖地牙哥	809
		Santo Domingo 聖多明哥	809
Egypt 埃及	20	Cairo 開羅	2
El Salvador 薩爾瓦多	503		
Finland 芬蘭	358	Helsinki 赫爾辛基	0
France 法國	33	Paris 巴黎	1
Germany 德國	49	Berlin 柏林	30
		Frankfurt Main 法蘭克福	69
		Hamburg 漢堡	40
		Munich 慕尼黑	89

Greece 希臘	30	Athens 雅典	1
Grenada 格瑞那達	1		809
Guam 關島	671		
Guatemala 瓜地馬拉	502		
Haiti 海地	509		
Honduras 宏都拉斯	504		
Hong Kong 香港	852		
Hungary 匈牙利	36	Budapest 布達佩斯	1
Iceland 冰島	354		
India 印度	91	Bombay 孟買	22
		New Delhi 新德里	11
Indonesia 印尼	62	Jakarta 雅加達	21
Iran 伊朗	98	Tehran 德黑蘭	21
Iraq Rep. 伊拉克	964	Baghdad 巴格達	1
Ireland 愛爾蘭	353	Dublin 都柏林	1
Israel 以色列	972	Jerusalem 耶路撒冷	2
		Tel Aviv 台拉維夫	3
Italy 義大利	39	Milan 米蘭	2
		Rome 羅馬	6
		Venice 威尼斯	41
Ivory Coast 象牙海岸	225		
Japan 日本	81	Kobe 神戶	78
		Kyoto 京都	75
		Nagoya 名古屋	52
		Osaka 大阪	6
		Tokyo 東京	3
		Yokohama 橫濱	45
Jordan 約旦	962	Amman 安曼	6
Kenya 肯亞	254	Nairobi 奈洛比	2
Korea, Rep. of 韓國	82	Pusan 釜山	51
		Seoul 漢城	2
Kuwait 科威特	965		
Lesotho 賴索托	266		
Liberia Rep. 賴比瑞亞	231		

Libya 利比亞	218	Tripoli 的黎波里	21
Macao 澳門	853		
Malawi 馬拉威	265		
Malaysia 馬來西亞	60	Kuala Lumpur 吉隆坡	3
		Penang 檳城	4
Mauritius 模里西斯	230		
Mexico 墨西哥	52	Mexico City 墨西哥城	5
Monaco 摩納哥	33		93
Nepal 尼泊爾	977	Katmandu 加德滿都	1
Netherlands 荷蘭	31	Amsterdam 阿姆斯特丹	20
		Rotterdam 鹿特丹	10
New Zealand 紐西蘭	64	Auckland 奧克蘭	9
		Wellington 威靈頓	4
Nicaragua 尼加拉瓜	505		
Nigeria 奈及利亞	234	Lagos 拉哥斯	1
Norway 挪威	47	Oslo 奧斯陸	2
Pakistan 巴基斯坦	92	Karachi 喀拉蚩	21
Panama 巴拿馬	507		
Paraguay 巴拉圭	595	Asuncion 亞松森	21
Peru 秘魯	51	Lima 利馬	14
Philippines 菲律賓	63	Manila 馬尼拉	2
Poland 波蘭	48	Warsaw 華沙	2 or 22
Portugal 葡萄牙	351	Lisbon 里斯本	1
Puerto Rico 波多黎各	1		809
Romania 羅馬尼亞	40	Bucharest 布加勒斯	0
Saudi Arabia 沙烏地阿拉伯	966	Jeddah 吉達	2
		Riyadh 利雅德	1
Singapore 新加坡	65		
South Africa 南非共和國	27	Johannesburg 約翰尼斯堡	1
Spain 西班牙	34	Madrid 馬德里	1
Swaziland 史瓦濟蘭	268		
Sweden 瑞典	46	Stockholm 斯德哥爾摩	8
Switzerland 瑞士	41	Geneva 日內瓦	22
		Zurich 蘇黎士	1

Taiwan 台灣	886	Taipei 台北	2
		Kaohsiung 高雄	7
Thailand 泰國	66	Bangkok 曼谷	2
		Chiang Mai 清邁	53
		Pattaya 普吉島	38
Tonga 東加	676		
Turkey 土耳其	90	Istanbul 伊斯坦堡	1
United Arab Emirates 阿拉伯聯合大公國	971	Dubai 杜拜	4
UK 英國	44	Liverpool 利物浦	51
		London 倫敦	71,81
		Manchester 曼徹斯特	61
Uruguay 烏拉圭	598	Montevideo 蒙特維多	2
USA 美國	1	Boston (MA) 波士頓	617
		Chicago (IL) 芝加哥	312
		Honolulu (HI) 檀香山	808
		Las Vegas (NV) 拉斯維加斯	702
		Los Angeles (CA) 洛杉磯	213
		"	714
		"	818
		New York (NY) 紐約	212
		"	718
		San Francisco (CA) 舊金山	415
		Seattle (WA) 西雅圖	206
		Washington (DC) 華聖頓	202
Russia 俄羅斯	7	Moscow 莫斯科	095
Vatican 梵諦岡	39		6
Venezuela 委內瑞拉	58	Caracas 卡拉卡斯	2
Vietnam 越南	84	Ho Chi Minh City 胡志民市	8
Yugoslavia 南斯拉夫	38	Belgrade 貝爾格勒	11

• 心得筆記欄 •

說英文高手 與傳統會話教材有何不同？

1. 我們學了那麼多年的英語會語，為什麼還不會說？

我們所使用的教材不對。傳統實況會話教材，如去郵局、在機場、看醫生等，勉強背下來，哪有機會使用？不使用就會忘記。等到有一天到了郵局，早就忘了你所學的。

2.「說英文高手」這本書，和傳統的英語會話教材有何不同？

「說英文高手」這本書，以三句為一組，任何時候都可以說，可以對外國人說，也可以和中國人說，有時可自言自語說。例如：你幾乎天天都可以說：What a beautiful day it is! It's not too hot. It's not too cold. It's just right. 傳統的英語會話教材，都是以兩個人以上的對話為主，主角又是你，又是別人，當然記不下來。「說英文高手」的主角就是你，先從你天天可說的話開始。把你要說的話用英文表達出來，所以容易記下來。

3. 為什麼用「說英文高手」這本書，學了馬上就會說？

書中的教材，學起來有趣，一次說三句，不容易忘記。例如：你有很多機會可以對朋友說：Never give up. Never give in. Never say never.

4. 傳統會話教材目標不明確，一句句學，學了後面，忘了前面，一輩子記不起來。「說英文高手」目標明確，先從一次說三句開始，自我訓練以後，能夠隨時說六句以上，例如：你說的話，別人不相信，傳統會話只教你一句：I'm not kidding. 連這句話你都會忘掉。「說英文高手」教你一次說很多句：

I mean what I say.
I say what I mean.
I really mean it.
I'm not kidding you.
I'm not joking with you.
I'm telling you the truth.

你唸唸看，背這六句是不是比背一句容易呢？能夠一次說六句以上英文，你會有無比興奮的感覺，當說英文變成你的愛好的時候，你的目標就達成。

全省各大書局均售 ◉ **書180元 / 錄音帶四卷500元**

✌️「**說英文高手**」為劉毅老師最新創作，是學習出版公司轟動全國的暢銷新書。
已被多所學校採用為會話教材。本書適合高中及大學使用，也適合自修。

國立中央圖書館出版品預行編目資料

新應用英文範例 / 吳濱伶編著　　　　--初版--
〔台北市〕：學習發行；
〔台北市〕：紅螞蟻總經銷，1995〔民84〕
　面；公分
ISBN 957-519-436-5（平裝）

1. 英國語言—應用文
805.179　　　　　　　　　　　　　　84003386

新應用英文範例

編　　著／吳　濱　伶
發　行　所／學習出版有限公司　　☎ (02) 2704-5525
郵　撥　帳　號／0512727-2 學習出版社帳戶
登　記　證／局版台業 2179 號
印　刷　所／裕強彩色印刷有限公司
台 北 門 市／台北市許昌街 10 號 2 F　　☎ (02) 2331-4060・2331-9209
台 中 門 市／台中市綠川東街 32 號 8 F 23 室　☎ (04) 223-2838
台灣總經銷／紅螞蟻圖書有限公司　　☎ (02) 2799-9490・2657-0132
美國總經銷／ Evergreen Book Store　　☎ (818) 2813622

售價：新台幣二百三十元正

2000 年 10 月 1 日一版三刷

ISBN 957-519-436-5